THE   BOOK   OF

ANTIPASTI

T H E   B O O K   O F

ANTIPASTI

LYN RUTHERFORD

Photographed by
PATRICK McLEAVEY

HPBooks
a division of
PRICE STERN SLOAN

ANOTHER BEST SELLING VOLUME FROM HPBOOKS

HPBooks
A division of Price Stern Sloan, Inc.
11150 Olympic Boulevard
Suite 650
Los Angeles, California 90064
9 8 7 6 5 4 3 2 1

By arrangement with Salamander Books Ltd.

This book was created by Patrick McLeavey & Partners,
21-22 Great Sutton Street, London EC1V 0DN

Art Director: Sue Storey
Editor: Hilaire Walden
Home Economist: Lyn Rutherford
Typeset by: Maron Graphics Ltd, Wembley
Colour separation by: Scantrans Pte. Ltd, Singapore
Printed in Belgium by Proost International Book Production

CONTENTS

INTRODUCTION

In Italian cooking Antipasti are appetizers or light starters which are served as the first course of a meal. The antipasti may be simply some sliced prosciutto or bread and olives, or there may be some fifteen or more tempting morsels to be sampled.

Cured meats and sausages are an important feature of antipasti, served on their own, with fresh fruit or with a simple olive and lemon juice dressing. Fish and shellfish are also popular favorites, particularly in the coastal areas of Italy. Bite-sized pieces are crumbed or lightly battered, fried and served hot with wedges of lemon for squeezing. Seafood salads have generous quantities of fruity olive oil dressings, which are soaked up with delicious Italian bread. Favorites such as squid, scallops, shrimp and mussels may be stuffed, grilled, baked, poached or fried. Cheeses and eggs are used in salads and dips, put on bread and into pastries. Vegetables are served raw in salads, or cooked and dressed with olive oil and fresh herbs.

A selection of antipasti dishes can make a meal in itself that is perfect for relaxed lunches and suppers and convivial dinner parties. Choose a range of dishes which give a good variety of flavors and textures and serve them with lots of warm crusty bread and plenty of Italian wine. Follow this with fresh fruit and cheese and finish the meal the Italian way with good, strong coffee.

INGREDIENTS

For the most part the recipes in this book call upon everyday ingredients. There are a few specialist ingredients, however, which are worth hunting for in Italian food stores to give your antipasti traditional, authentic flavors.

STORE CUPBOARD INGREDIENTS

Olive oil—the best quality is cold pressed 'Extra Virgin Olive Oil'. Arguably the best source is said to be Lucca in Tuscany but, rather like wine, olive oil will vary from individual groves and from year to year. For salads use rich, green extra-virgin olive oil (as a general rule the greener the color the richer and fruitier the flavor) but for cooking you can use a less expensive olive oil with a blander flavor which will not dominate the other flavors in a dish, or use a mixture of olive oil and either peanut or sunflower oil. A good quality olive oil can easily be flavored to give an added dimension to dressings and sauces. Try adding ingredients such as garlic, fresh herbs, lemon peel, chiles, peppercorns or other spices. A traditional example of this is 'Olio Santo' (Holy Oil) where the best extra-virgin olive oil is flavored with fresh basil and hot red chile peppers.

Olives—green olives are unripe, black ones fully ripe, you can buy them preserved in brine or in oil. They are widely available in many forms—pitted or unpitted, or stuffed with ingredients such as pimentos, anchovy fillets or almonds.

Olive paste—made from green or ripe olives ground to a paste with a little olive oil and seasonings. Olive paste can be bought in jars from supermarkets, delicatessens and Italian food stores, but it is very easy to make yourself. Simply process pitted olives in a blender or food processor, adding seasoning and just enough good quality oil to make a fairly smooth paste. Store in small jars, keep fresh and airtight by covering with a layer of olive oil. (A small jar prepared in this way can be kept, refrigerated, for about 1 month). Olive paste is delicious as a snack or simple antipasto on toast, tossed with pasta or cooked vegetables, or served as a dip.

Balsamic vinegar—more expensive than wine vinegars, but with a rich, sweet aromatic flavor. The price will vary enormously according to the length of time the vinegar has been matured. The more mature vinegars are more concentrated and so can be used very sparingly. A few drops is often all that is required to flavor a dressing.

Sun-dried tomatoes—when these are specified in a recipe those packed in oil in jars have been used. Their concentrated, salty, tomato flavor is good in salads, on bread with cheeses, and chopped into dressings and dips. Sun-dried tomatoes can also be bought loose in the dry state but they will need to be reconstituted before they are used. Put the pieces of tomato in a bowl, pour over boiling water and leave 1 to 1-1/2 hours; they will soften but still be chewy. Drain well and dry on paper towels.

Sun-dried tomato paste—with a richer flavor than ordinary tomato paste, sun-dried tomato paste is a really useful cupboard ingredient. It transforms sauces and soups and makes a quick pizza topping. Used sparingly with basil and garlic, it becomes a sauce for pasta and makes a superb savory when thinly spread on hot toasted bread.

Capers in wine vinegar—have a sharp aromatic flavor that is a perfect contrast to oily fish, eggs, fried and rich foods. Look for those preserved in wine vinegar as others can have a harsh, vinegary taste.

Red and yellow bell peppers in wine vinegar—have a sweet sour flavor. They are a useful cupboard stand-by as it is easy to use just a small piece as a garnish, cut into strips or dice. The vinegar can be used as a flavoring.

Porcini (dried ceps)—are essential for all mushroom recipes where the strong, earthy flavor of wild mushrooms is desired. Buy porcini in small packets (a little goes a long way) from Italian delicatessens and use in rice dishes, sautées and stuffings. To reconstitute before using, put the porcini in a small bowl, pour over boiling water and leave 20 to 30 minutes. Drain, reserving the soaking liquor, then rinse the porcini. Chop them for use. Use the soaking liquor, as a wonderful mushroomy stock.

1 *Sun-dried tomatoes;* 2 *Sun-dried tomato paste;* 3 *Porcini mushrooms;* 4 *Red and yellow bell peppers in wine vinegar;* 5 *Capers;* 6 *Stuffed olives;* 7 *Ripe olive paste;* 8 *Green olive paste;* 9 *Green and ripe olives.*

CHEESE

Mozzarella—true mozzarella is made from buffalo milk, but today most of what we buy is made from cows' milk. This is fine for cooked dishes, on pizzas and with pasta, but for salads or for eating on its own as a dessert cheese it is worth paying more for full-flavored, more creamy textured mozzarella di bufala.

Parmesan—the most famous matured hard cheese of Italy, Parmesan is most often used for grating over pasta, risottos, sauces and other cooked dishes, but it is also superb in salads and as a table cheese. Always buy Parmesan in a piece to be cut or grated as needed.

The drums of ready-grated Parmesan cheese that are available simply do not compare in flavor.

Pecorino—is a hard cheese which has a fairly strong distinctive taste. It is used and eaten in the same way as Parmesan. Pecorino is available in several varieties such as Pecorino Sardo, made in Sardinia; Pecorino Romano; Pecorino Toscano; and Pecorino Pepato which is spiced with peppercorns.

Provolone—is made in a variety of shapes such as oval, cone and pear shapes which are hung by cords to ripen. Young mild 'provolone dolce' is most often eaten as a table cheese while the stronger, mature 'provolone piccante' is usually used in cooking.

Fontina—a semi-hard cheese with a natural brown rind, creamy texture and a sweet, nutty flavor. Fontina is considered a fine table cheese but it is also a good cooking cheese and its popular use is in the hot cheese fondue of the Piedmont region, 'Fonduta'.

Gorgonzola—a blue-veined cheese with a pleasantly sharp flavor made in the town of the same name in the Lombardy region of Italy.

Dolcelatte—is a factory made version of Gorgonzola. It has a milder, sweeter flavor as its name suggests—dolcelatte translates to 'sweet milk'.

Mascarpone—a fresh unripened cheese made from curdling thick cream with citric acid, heating and whipping it. It is very rich, and has a thick velvety texture. Mascarpone is available in containers in some supermarkets and delicatessens. It is often served sweetened and flavored with liqueurs as a dessert but its luxurious flavor and texture are good in savory dishes too.

SAUSAGES AND CURED MEATS

Salami—there are countless varieties of Italian salami, each region having its own specialities. Italian salamis are made of raw ingredients which are cured by brine-pickling and/or smoking. The following examples are

1 *Ricotta*; 2 *Mozzarella*; 3 *Dolcelatte*; 4 *Fontina*; 5 *Parmesan*; 6 *Provolone*; 7 *Pecorino di Sardo*; 8 *Mascarpone*; 9 *Pecorino*.

1 *Italian pork sausages*; 2 *Prosciutto*; 3 *Coppa di Parma*; 4 *Salami (Felino)*; 5 *Salami
(Napoli)*; 6 *Bresaola*; 7 *Mortadella*.

available outside Italy and are well
worth looking for in delicatessens and
Italian food shops.

Milano—fairly fine in texture, this large
salami, is made from minced pork or a
mixture of pork and beef.

Varzi—coarse and highly spiced and
seasoned, this salami is produced in the
village of Varzi in the Parma region.

Felino—a long, thin, pork salami,
coarse in texture with a good flavor.
Felino is always sliced on the diagonal.

Finocchiona—a large, pure pork salami
distinctively flavored with fennel
seeds. It comes from Tuscany.

Prosciutto—salted and air-dried raw
pork. Parma ham is the most famous of
these cured meats but other regions
produce their own versions.

Bresaola—sold thinly sliced, bresaola
is raw beef which has been salted and
air-dried in the same way as prosciutto.

Coppa di Parma—like prosciutto di
Parma this is salted and air-dried raw
pork but it is the shoulder cut rather
than the hind leg. The flavor is slightly
sweeter than prosciutto.

Mortadella—the largest and probably
the most famous Italian sausage. The
best mortadella is made from pure pork
but others may contain some beef or
organ meats. The spices and flavorings
can vary and mortadella may contain
whole black peppercorns, coriander
seeds, pitted olives or pistachio nuts.
It is usually served very thinly sliced,
but it may also be diced and added to
salads or cooked dishes.

——— BEAN & ONION SALAD ———

12 ounces green beans
1 onion, thinly sliced
2 tablespoons capers in wine vinegar, drained
6 tablespoons extra-virgin olive oil
Juice of 1 lemon
1/2 teaspoon hot red pepper flakes
Pinch of sugar
Salt and freshly ground pepper
2 teaspoons chopped Italian parsley
1 teaspoon chopped mint

Add beans to a saucepan of boiling salted water and cook 4 minutes until tender. Drain and refresh under cold running water. Place in a bowl with onion and capers.

Beat olive oil, lemon juice, red pepper flakes, sugar, salt and freshly ground pepper in a small bowl or shake together in a jar with a tight-fitting lid.

Pour over salad, add herbs and mix well.

Makes 4 to 6 servings.

—ASPARAGUS & EGG SALAD—

2 pound asparagus
Salt and freshly ground pepper
7 hard-cooked eggs
6 tablespoons olive oil
2 tablespoons white wine vinegar
2 small dill pickles, finely chopped
Freshly ground pepper
Chopped Italian parsley and Italian parsley sprig
   to garnish

Snap off and discard woody ends of asparagus stems. Using a small sharp knife, scrape stems. Rinse asparagus, then tie into small bundles using string.

Stand bundles in a deep pan of boiling salted water so tips are above water. Cover, making a dome of foil, if necessary. Boil 15 minutes until tips are crisp-tender. Drain, refresh under cold running water, drain, untie bundles and cool.

Finely chop 4 of the eggs and place in a bowl. Using a wooden spoon, gradually stir in oil, vinegar and pickles. Season with salt and freshly ground pepper. Set aside. Quarter remaining eggs and arrange with asparagus around edge of a serving plate. Pour egg sauce into center and sprinkle with chopped Italian parsley. Garnish with Italian parsley sprig.

Makes 4 to 6 servings.

BELL PEPPER SALAD

1 large red bell pepper
1 large green bell pepper
1 large yellow bell pepper
1 small red onion, sliced
16 ripe olives
2 teaspoons chopped basil or 2/3 teaspoon dried leaf
 basil
2 teaspoons chopped thyme or 2/3 teaspoon dried leaf
 thyme
DRESSING:
3 tablespoons extra-virgin olive oil
1 tablespoon red wine vinegar
1 garlic clove, finely chopped
Pinch of sugar
Salt and freshly ground pepper

To make dressing, mix all ingredients together in a small bowl, or shake together in a jar with a tight-fitting lid. Set aside. Preheat broiler. Place whole peppers under hot broiler about 10 minutes, turning occasionally, until skins are evenly blistered and blackened. Transfer peppers to a plastic bag a few minutes, then peel away and discard skins.

Cut peppers in half, remove and discard seeds and cut peppers into strips. Place in a salad bowl with onion and olives. Stir or shake dressing and pour over salad. Toss gently to mix and sprinkle with herbs.

Makes 4 servings.

— MUSHROOMS & LIMA BEANS —

1-1/3 cups dried lima beans, soaked overnight, and
 drained
3 cups thinly sliced button mushrooms
2-ounce piece Parmesan cheese
1 tablespoon finely chopped Italian parsley
Lettuce leaves and Italian parsley sprigs to garnish
DRESSING:
5 tablespoons extra-virgin olive oil
Finely grated peel of 1/2 lemon
1/2 teaspoon whole-grain mustard
Pinch of sugar
Salt and freshly ground pepper

Put beans in a large saucepan with enough
water to cover. Bring to a boil and boil briskly
10 minutes, then reduce heat and simmer 40
to 45 minutes or until beans are tender. Drain
and rinse under cold running water. Drain
well and leave until cold. To make dressing,
mix all ingredients together in a small bowl or
shake together a jar with a tight-fitting lid.
Set aside.

Put beans and mushrooms in a large serving
bowl. Add dressing and toss well to mix.
Let stand up to 2 hours, if desired. Using a
small, sharp knife, pare wafer-thin slices of
cheese, add to salad and toss lightly to mix.
Sprinkle with chopped Italian parsley,
garnish with lettuce leaves and Italian parsley
sprigs and serve immediately.

Makes 6 servings.

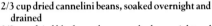

MIXED BEAN SALAD

2/3 cup dried cannelini beans, soaked overnight and
  drained
2/3 cup dried black-eyed peas, soaked overnight and
  drained
2/3 cup dried lima beans, soaked overnight and drained
1 small onion, chopped
2 tablespoons chopped oregano or 2 teaspoons dried
  leaf oregano
1 tablespoon chopped Italian parsley
Italian parsley sprig to garnish
DRESSING:
1/4 cup extra-virgin olive oil
2 tablespoons red wine vinegar
2 garlic cloves, crushed
Salt and freshly ground pepper

Place beans in separate pans. Cover with cold
water, bring to a boil and boil briskly 10
minutes, then reduce heat and simmer,
covered, about 1 hour until just tender.
Drain, rinse briefly under cold running water,
then drain and transfer to a serving dish.

To make dressing, mix all ingredients together in a small bowl or shake together in a
jar with a tight-fitting lid. Add onion and
dressing to beans while they are warm. Stir
and cool to room temperature. Cover and
chill until served. Just before serving, stir in
oregano and parsley and adjust seasoning.
Garnish with Italian parsley sprig.

Makes 6 servings.

── RICE-STUFFED TOMATOES ──

6 large, ripe tomatoes
2/3 cup risotto rice or long-grain white rice
1-1/2 cups boiling chicken stock
4 tablespoons olive oil
1 small onion, finely chopped
1 garlic clove, crushed
1/2 pound fresh spinach, finely chopped
3 tablespoons chopped Italian parsley or fennel
Salt and freshly ground pepper
Mixed lettuce leaves to serve

Cut tops off tomatoes and reserve. Using a teaspoon scoop out seeds and flesh from tomatoes; reserve seeds and flesh for use in sauces or casseroles.

Place tomatoes upside down to drain. Preheat oven to 350F (175C). Rinse rice and put in a small saucepan with boiling chicken stock. Bring to a boil, then reduce heat, cover and simmer 12 to 15 minutes until liquid is absorbed. If rice is not tender, stir in a little boiling water and continue cooking. Meanwhile, heat 2 tablespoons of the oil in a medium-size saucepan. Add onion and garlic and saute 3 minutes to soften.

Stir in spinach, parsley or fennel and cooked rice. Remove from heat and season with salt and freshly ground pepper. Sprinkle insides of tomatoes with a little salt and fill with rice mixture. Replace reserved tomato tops. Arrange in a baking dish and sprinkle with remaining oil. Bake in the preheated oven 20 minutes until tomatoes are tender. Serve hot or cold with lettuce leaves.

Makes 6 servings.

──EGGPLANT NAPOLETANA──

1-1/2 pounds medium-size Japanese-type eggplant
Salt
1 cup all-purpose flour
1 cup peanut oil
1 cup olive oil
1/2 cup extra-virgin olive oil
6 anchovy fillets in oil, drained and mashed
1 tablespoon sun-dried tomato paste
3 tablespoons red wine vinegar
8 Italian parsley sprigs
2 garlic cloves
Freshly ground pepper
Italian parsley sprigs to garnish

Peel the eggplants and cut into 1-inch slices. Spread eggplant out on a large plate and sprinkle with salt. Leave 30 minutes, then rinse thoroughly under cold running water to remove salt, drain and pat dry with paper towels.

Put flour into a large plastic bag, add eggplant and toss to coat. Remove coated eggplant and discard excess flour.

Preheat peanut oil and olive oil together in a saucepan or deep-fryer to 375F (190C). Deep-fry eggplant in batches in the hot oil about 4 minutes until golden-brown. Transfer to paper towels to drain. Keep hot.

In a small saucepan, gently warm the extra-virgin oil over low heat. Stir in anchovies, tomato paste and vinegar and simmer, stirring, 2 minutes.

Finely chop together the parsley sprigs and garlic. Transfer eggplant to a warmed serving plate. Top with anchovy sauce and season with salt and freshly ground pepper. Sprinkle with chopped parsley and garlic and serve immediately garnished with Italian parsley sprigs.

Makes 4 to 6 servings.

— BROCCOLI & PROSCIUTTO —

1-1/2 pounds broccoli
1/2 pound tomatoes
3 tablespoons olive oil
5 ounces prosciutto, cut into strips
2 garlic cloves, chopped
1/3 cup pine nuts, toasted
12 pitted ripe olives, halved
Salt and freshly ground pepper
Handful of basil leaves

Divide the broccoli into flowerets. Add to a saucepan of boiling salted water and cook about 4 minutes, until crisp-tender. Drain, refresh under cold running water, then drain well.

Meanwhile, put tomatoes in a bowl and add boiling water to cover. Leave about 30 seconds, then drain, cool with cold water and peel away skins. Cut the tomatoes into chunks and discard the seeds. Heat 2 tablespoons of the oil in a skillet. Add prosciutto and garlic and cook over high heat 2 to 3 minutes until prosciutto is crisp. Using a slotted spoon transfer prosciutto to a plate and keep warm.

Add remaining oil to pan with tomatoes, pine nuts and olives. Cook, stirring, 1 minute. Stir in broccoli and prosciutto and heat through briefly, gently stirring. Season with salt and freshly ground pepper. Transfer to a warmed serving dish and sprinkle with basil leaves. Serve hot.

Makes 4 to 6 servings.

— BAKED STUFFED ARTICHOKES —

4 large artichokes
1 tablespoon butter
5 tablespoons olive oil
3 slices lean bacon, chopped
1 small onion, finely chopped
2 celery stalks, finely chopped
2 medium-size zucchini, finely chopped
1 garlic clove, crushed
1 tablespoon chopped sage or 1 teaspoon dried sage
1 tablespoon chopped Italian parsley
Salt and freshly ground pepper
3 tablespoons fresh bread crumbs
1/4 cup shredded pecorino cheese (1 ounce)
Juice of 1 lemon
Italian parsley sprigs to garnish

Preheat oven to 400F (205C). Cook artichokes in a saucepan of boiling salted water 30 minutes. Remove and place upside down to drain. Pull away and discard outer leaves and, using a teaspoon, remove central hairy choke. Heat butter and 2 tablespoons of the olive oil in a saucepan. Add bacon, onion, celery, zucchini and garlic and cook 5 minutes, stirring frequently, until vegetables are just soft. Stir in herbs. Puree half the mixture in a blender or food processor fitted with the metal blade. Return to pan. Season with salt and freshly ground pepper.

Place artichokes close together in baking dish. Fill center of artichokes with vegetable mixture. In a small bowl, mix together bread crumbs and cheese. Pile on top of filling. Sprinkle with lemon juice and remaining 3 tablespoons olive oil. Cover with foil and bake in preheated oven 15 minutes. Remove foil. Bake 10 minutes until lightly browned. Garnish with Italian parsley sprigs.

Makes 4 servings.

STUFFED ARTICHOKE BOTTOMS

6 hard-cooked eggs, finely chopped
7 to 9 tablespoons extra-virgin olive oil
2 tablespoons white wine vinegar
1/2 red bell pepper packed in wine vinegar, drained and chopped
2 tablespoons capers in wine vinegar, drained and chopped
2 tablespoons chopped Italian parsley
Salt and freshly ground pepper
1 (14-oz) can artichoke bottoms, drained
3 tablespoons extra-virgin olive oil
Juice of 1/2 lemon
1 teaspoon coriander seeds, crushed
Italian parsley sprigs to garnish

Place eggs in a bowl then, using a wooden spoon, gradually stir in 4 tablespoons of the oil and the vinegar; the mixture should be stiff enough to hold its shape but if too dry add a little more olive oil. Stir in bell pepper, capers and parsley and season with salt and freshly ground pepper.

Divide egg mixture among artichoke bottoms and arrange on a serving plate. Drizzle with the 3 tablespoons olive oil and lemon juice and sprinkle with coriander seeds. Cover and refrigerate at least 1 hour. Serve garnished with Italian parsley sprigs.

Makes 4 to 6 servings.

—— CAULIFLOWER INSALATA ——

1 cauliflower
1/3 cup pitted green olives, halved
1/3 cup pitted ripe olives, halved
2 tablespoons capers in wine vinegar, drained
1 red bell pepper packed in wine vinegar, drained and
    chopped
5 anchovy fillets canned in oil, drained and halved
    crosswise
6 tablespoons extra-virgin olive oil
1 tablespoon white wine vinegar
Salt and freshly ground pepper
3 small carrots

Break the cauliflower into flowerets.

Add cauliflower to a saucepan of boiling salted water and boil 4 to 5 minutes until crisp-tender. Drain, refresh under cold running water, drain again and cool. Put into a serving bowl with olives, capers, bell pepper and anchovies. Add oil and vinegar and season with salt and freshly ground pepper. Toss gently to mix and refrigerate at least 30 minutes.

Using a vegetable peeler, remove long thin slices from carrots. Place slices in a bowl of iced water 10 minutes to curl and crisp. Drain thoroughly and add to salad. Toss lightly to mix, then serve.

Makes 6 servings.

FUNGHETTO

1 eggplant (about 8 ounces), diced
2 cups thinly sliced zucchini (about 8 ounces)
Salt
1/2 ounce dried porcini mushrooms
2 tablespoons butter
1/4 cup olive oil
2 garlic cloves, crushed
4 cups sliced button or oyster mushrooms or a mixture
    (8 ounces)
2 tablespoons rosemary leaves
2 tablespoons chopped Italian parsley
Freshly ground pepper
Rosemary sprig to garnish

Put eggplant and zucchini into a colander. Sprinkle with salt and drain 30 minutes.

Rinse thoroughly to remove salt and drain on paper towels. Put dried mushrooms into a small bowl. Cover with warm water and soak 20 minutes. Strain, reserving 3 tablespoons soaking liquid. Rinse thoroughly and chop.

Heat butter and oil in a large heavy skillet. Add garlic and saute 1 minute. Add eggplant, zucchini, fresh and dried mushrooms and rosemary. Saute 3 to 4 minutes. Stir in reserved porcini soaking liquor and the parsley, reduce heat and cook 20 minutes until vegetables are soft and liquid evaporated. Season with salt and freshly ground pepper. Garnish with rosemary sprig.

Makes 4 to 6 servings.

—— ZUCCHINI WITH GARLIC ——

6 medium-size zucchini
1 cup corn oil or peanut oil
1 cup light olive oil
2 garlic cloves, finely chopped
1/3 cup red wine vinegar
1 to 2 tablespoons chopped dill
Salt and freshly ground pepper
12 mint leaves

Preheat oven to 375F (190C). Using a vegetable peeler and pressing quite firmly, peel
along the length of the zucchini to remove
long thick strips. Divide between 2 baking
sheets; bake 20 minutes until crisp-tender.

Transfer zucchini to paper towels to drain 30
minutes. Preheat the oils together in a saucepan or deep-fryer to 375F (190C). Line a
baking sheet with paper towels. Fry zucchini
slices in batches in the hot oil 2 to 3 minutes
until light golden-brown. Transfer to paper
towels to drain. When all the zucchini are
cooked and drained transfer to a serving dish.

Add garlic, wine vinegar, dill, salt and freshly
ground pepper to zucchini. Toss gently to
mix. Cover and refrigerate at least 2 hours.
Serve sprinkled with mint leaves.

Makes 6 servings.

–MUSHROOMS WITH MARSALA–

1/4 cup butter
6 cups thickly sliced large button mushrooms
  (about 1 pound)
2 garlic cloves, sliced
2/3 cup marsala wine
Salt and freshly ground pepper
Chopped Italian parsley and Italian parsley leaves
  to garnish

Preheat oven to 375F (190C). Use butter to grease a large flat baking dish.

Layer mushrooms in dish and sprinkle with garlic.

Pour marsala over mushrooms and season with salt and freshly ground pepper. Bake in preheated oven 25 to 30 minutes until mushrooms are tender. Serve hot or cold sprinkled with chopped Italian parsley and Italian parsley leaves.

Makes 4 servings.

Note: For a special occasion or a treat, substitute fresh porcini mushrooms for some of the button mushrooms.

ZUCCHINI-MUSHROOM FRITTERS

6 small zucchini with flowers
6 ounces oyster mushrooms
1/4 cup balsamic vinegar
1/4 cup extra-virgin olive oil
1 tablespoon chopped basil or 1 teaspoon dried leaf basil
Salt and freshly ground pepper
Sifted all-purpose flour for coating
Peanut oil for deep-frying
Salt
Basil leaves to garnish
BATTER:
1 egg, lightly beaten
1 cup ice-cold water
About 1 cup all-purpose flour, sifted

Break flowers off zucchini.

Slice each zucchini lengthwise into three strips. Cut large mushrooms into halves or quarters; leave others whole. Place vinegar in a small bowl for dipping. In a separate small bowl mix together olive oil, basil, salt and freshly ground pepper. Set both aside. To make batter, in a small bowl, stir together egg and water. Gently mix in enough flour to give batter the consistency of light cream.

Half fill a deep-fryer or saucepan with oil and preheat to 350F (175C). Dip zucchini strips and flowers and mushrooms into sifted flour to coat. Shake off excess. Dip a few pieces of floured vegetables at a time in batter, then deep-fry in hot oil 3 to 4 minutes, turning frequently, until golden. Drain on paper towels. Season with salt. Garnish with basil leaves. Serve with the bowls of balsamic vinegar and flavored oil.

Makes 4 to 6 servings.

PEPERONATA

2 green bell peppers
1 red bell pepper
1/3 cup olive oil
1 onion, coarsely chopped
1 garlic clove, crushed
1-1/2 pounds tomatoes, peeled, seeded and chopped
Pinch of sugar
Salt and freshly ground pepper
1 tablespoon chopped Italian parsley
Italian parsley sprig to garnish

Preheat broiler. Place whole peppers under hot broiler about 10 minutes, turning occasionally, until skins are evenly blistered and blackened.

Transfer to a plastic bag a few minutes, then peel away and discard skins. Cut peppers in half, remove and discard seeds and cut peppers into strips. Heat oil in a large skillet over medium heat. Add onion and garlic and cook 3 minutes to soften. Stir in tomatoes and sugar and cook 10 to 12 minutes until thickened.

Add pepper strips and simmer 5 minutes until peppers are soft. Season with salt and freshly ground pepper and serve hot sprinkled with chopped Italian parsley and garnished with Italian parsley sprig.

Makes 4 servings.

– ARUGULA & PINE NUT SALAD –

1/3 cup pine nuts
4 ounces arugula
4 green onions, thinly sliced
8 chervil sprigs, coarsely torn
2 thin slices prosciutto, cut into strips
DRESSING:
Juice of 1 lemon
3 tablespoons extra-virgin olive oil
1 tablespoon walnut oil
1/2 teaspoon Dijon-style mustard
Salt and freshly ground pepper

In a small saucepan, heat the pine nuts over medium-high heat, stirring constantly, about 3 minutes until golden-brown.

Remove to a plate and set aside to cool. Place arugula, green onions and chervil in a serving bowl. Toss gently to mix.

To make dressing, mix ingredients together in a small bowl or shake together in a jar with a tight-fitting lid. Pour over salad and toss. Sprinkle with reserved pine nuts.

Makes 4 to 6 servings.

-TOMATO & RED ONION SALAD-

4 beefsteak tomatoes, sliced
4 sun-dried tomatoes packed in oil, drained and
   chopped
1 red onion, chopped
Salt and freshly ground pepper
3 tablespoons extra-virgin olive oil
2 tablespoons oil from the sun-dried tomatoes
2 tablespoons red wine vinegar
Pinch of sugar
4 tablespoons chopped mixed fresh herbs such as basil,
   oregano, parsley, chives, dill and cilantro
Herb sprigs to garnish

Layer tomatoes, sun-dried tomatoes and
onion in a shallow serving dish. Season with
salt and freshly ground pepper.

Mix together remaining ingredients except
herb sprigs in a small bowl, then pour over
salad. Garnish with herb sprigs.

Makes 4 to 6 servings.

BAKED STUFFED CELERY

1 head celery separated into stalks and cut into 3-inch
   lengths
1/4 cup olive oil
STUFFING:
3 tablespoons olive oil
1 small onion, finely chopped
1 garlic clove, chopped
2 tablespoons capers in wine vinegar, drained
1 red bell pepper packed in wine vinegar, drained and
   chopped
1/2 cup fresh bread crumbs
1/2 cup grated provolone cheese (2 ounces)
3 tablespoons chopped Italian parsley
Salt and freshly ground pepper
Italian parsley to garnish

Preheat oven to 375F (190C). Add celery to
a large saucepan of boiling water and cook 3
minutes. Drain and refresh under cold running water. Drain on paper towels. To make
stuffing, heat oil in a skillet. Add onion and
garlic and cook 3 minutes to soften. Remove
from heat. Chop together capers and bell
pepper, then stir into skillet with bread
crumbs, cheese and the 3 tablespoons parsley.
Season with salt and freshly ground pepper.

Place stuffing in cavities of celery pieces.
Arrange celery with stuffing up, in one layer
in a shallow baking dish. Drizzle with oil.
Cover with foil and bake in preheated oven
20 minutes. Remove foil and continue cooking about 10 minutes until celery is tender
and stuffing lightly browned. Serve hot or
warm, garnished with Italian parsley.

Makes 6 servings.

TRICOLOR SALAD

1 avocado
2 tablespoons lemon juice
2 large beefsteak tomatoes, sliced
6 ounces Italian mozzarella cheese, preferably made
   from buffalo milk
Salt and freshly ground pepper
Few drops balsamic vinegar
1/4 cup extra-virgin olive oil
6 fresh basil leaves, shredded
Basil sprigs to garnish

Seed and peel avocado, slice thinly and brush
with lemon juice.

Arrange tomatoes, cheese and avocado on a
large plate. Season with salt and freshly
ground pepper.

Drizzle balsamic vinegar and oil over salad;
sprinkle with shredded basil. Garnish with
basil sprigs.

Makes 4 to 6 servings.

—ZUCCHINI & TOMATO SALAD—

About 30 (2-inch-long) zucchini (about 1 pound total)
12 ounces small tomatoes, sliced
4 green onions, white part only, finely chopped
1 tablespoon chopped Italian parsley
Italian parsley sprig to garnish
DRESSING:
5 tablespoons extra-virgin olive oil
3 tablespoons white wine vinegar
2 garlic cloves, chopped
1 tablespoon chopped thyme or 1 teaspoon dried leaf
   thyme
1 teaspoon honey
Salt and freshly ground pepper

Add zucchini to a saucepan of boiling salted water and cook 3 minutes. Drain well. Using a small, sharp knife, cut a long lengthwise slit in each zucchini, place in a serving dish.

To make dressing, mix ingredients together in a small bowl or shake together in a jar with a tight-fitting lid. Pour over hot zucchini and leave until completely cold. Add tomatoes, green onions and parsley to dish. Toss to mix. Adjust seasoning before serving. Garnish with Italian parsley sprig.

Makes 6 servings.

—FENNEL & DOLCELATTE—

3 medium-size fennel bulbs
1 tablespoon fennel seeds, lightly crushed
1/4 cup extra-virgin olive oil
Juice of 1/2 lemon
Pinch of sugar
Salt and freshly ground pepper
1 cup crumbled dolcelatte cheese

Trim fennel, reserving green feathery tops. Add whole bulbs to saucepan of boiling salted water. Cook 5 minutes, then drain. Refresh under cold running water, drain well and pat dry with paper towels. Set aside. Chop reserved fennel tops and set aside.

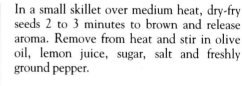

In a small skillet over medium heat, dry-fry seeds 2 to 3 minutes to brown and release aroma. Remove from heat and stir in olive oil, lemon juice, sugar, salt and freshly ground pepper.

Thinly slice fennel bulbs and arrange in a shallow serving dish. Add oil and fennel seed mixture. Sprinkle with cheese and reserved fennel tops. Let stand 30 minutes. Toss lightly before serving.

Makes 4 to 6 servings.

—EGG & ARTICHOKE SALAD—

4 hard-cooked eggs, quartered
12 artichoke hearts in oil, drained
12 stuffed green olives, halved
2 tablespoons capers in wine vinegar, drained
1 tablespoon chopped Italian parsley
1 tablespoon chopped oregano or 1 teaspoon dried leaf
  oregano
Italian parsley leaves to garnish
DRESSING:
5 tablespoons extra-virgin olive oil
2 tablespoons white wine vinegar
1 teaspoon Dijon-style mustard
1 teaspoon finely grated lemon peel
1 teaspoon honey
Salt and freshly ground pepper

Arrange eggs on a serving plate with artichokes and olives. Sprinkle with capers and
herbs.

To make dressing, mix all ingredients together in a small bowl, or shake together in a
jar with a tight-fitting lid. Pour over salad and
serve at once garnished with Italian parsley
leaves.

Makes 4 to 6 servings.

Note: Artichoke hearts in oil are similar, but
far superior, to canned artichoke hearts.
They are available at Italian delicatessens.

EGGPLANT WITH TOMATO SAUCE

8 to 10 small Japanese-type eggplant (about 1 pound total)
Salt
6 tablespoons extra-virgin olive oil
1 shallot, finely chopped
2 garlic cloves, crushed
1 pound tomatoes, peeled and finely chopped
2 oregano sprigs
1/3 cup red wine
1 tablespoon sun-dried tomato paste
1 tablespoon chopped Italian parsley
Freshly ground pepper
Italian parsley sprigs or basil sprigs to garnish

Leaving stem end intact, slice eggplant lengthwise from blossom end almost to stem end 3 or 4 times so they can be flattened out to give a fanned appearance.

Place in a shallow dish, sprinkle with salt and leave 25 to 30 minutes. Rinse thoroughly to remove salt. Drain and pat dry with paper towels; set aside. Preheat broiler.

Meanwhile, heat 2 tablespoons of the oil in a small saucepan, add shallot and garlic and cook 3 to 4 minutes to soften. Stir in tomatoes and oregano and cook 1 minute.

Add wine and tomato paste and bring to a boil. Reduce heat and simmer sauce, covered, 10 minutes, stirring frequently until vegetables are tender. Discard oregano, stir in parsley and season with salt and freshly ground pepper.

Arrange eggplant on a baking sheet. Press each eggplant to fan out slices. Brush with remaining 4 tablespoons olive oil and cook under hot broiler 5 to 6 minutes, turning once, until tender and beginning to brown. Serve immediately with hot sauce. Garnish with Italian parsley or basil sprigs.

Makes 4 to 6 servings.

—EGGPLANT & OLIVE SALAD—

2 Japanese-type eggplants, diced
Peanut oil for deep-frying
6 tablespoons light olive oil
2 onions, chopped
1 garlic clove, chopped
4 celery stalks, sliced
2 small zucchini, sliced
1 tablespoon chopped rosemary
1 (14-oz.) can chopped plum tomatoes
1 tablespoon sun-dried tomato paste
2 teaspoons sugar
1/3 cup red wine vinegar
1 cup pitted mixed olives, halved
2 tablespoons capers in wine vinegar, drained
Salt and freshly ground pepper
Italian parsley sprig to garnish

Put eggplant in a colander, sprinkle with salt and drain 30 to 40 minutes. Rinse thoroughly to remove salt, drain and pat dry with paper towels. Heat peanut oil in a large skillet over high heat. Add eggplant and fry 4 to 5 minutes until an even golden-brown. Transfer eggplant to paper towels. Transfer to a serving dish and set aside. Heat olive oil in a large skillet over medium heat, add onions and garlic and cook 5 minutes to soften.

Add celery, zucchini and rosemary and cook 5 minutes. Stir in plum tomatoes, tomato paste, sugar and vinegar and cook, stirring frequently, 10 minutes until vinegar has evaporated. Transfer to serving dish and cool. Add olives and capers to serving dish. Season with salt and freshly ground pepper and toss well to mix. Cover and refrigerate before serving. Garnish with Italian parsley sprig.

Makes 4 to 6 servings.

——CANNELINI BEAN PASTE——

1-1/4 cups dried cannelini beans, soaked overnight,
  drained
4 cups water
1/2 teaspoon hot red pepper flakes
2 teaspoons tomato paste
2 rosemary sprigs
2 tablespoons butter
2 tablespoons extra-virgin olive oil
1 garlic clove, finely chopped
1 tablespoon finely chopped oregano or 1 teaspoon
  dried leaf oregano
3/4 to 1 cup hot chicken stock
Juice of 1 small lemon
Salt and freshly ground pepper
Rosemary sprigs to garnish
Toasted bread or vegetable sticks to serve

Combine beans in a saucepan with the water, red pepper flakes, tomato paste and rosemary sprigs. Bring to a boil, then reduce heat, cover and simmer 2 hours until most of the water has been absorbed and beans are very tender. Discard rosemary. In a blender or food processor fitted with the metal blade, puree beans and remaining liquid until very smooth.

Heat butter and oil in a medium-size sauce-pan. Add garlic and oregano. Cook 2 minutes. Stir in bean puree and hot stock and simmer 10 to 12 minutes, stirring frequently, until mixture is very thick. Remove from heat, stir in lemon juice and season with salt and freshly ground pepper. Garnish with rosemary sprigs. Serve either hot spread on toasted crusty bread or cold with fresh vege-table sticks or warmed crusty bread.

Makes 6 servings.

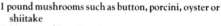

— MARINATED MUSHROOMS —

1 pound mushrooms such as button, porcini, oyster or
  shiitake
1-1/4 cups white wine vinegar
1-1/4 cups water
2 small fresh red chiles, halved lengthwise and seeded
Grated peel of 1 lemon
2 bay leaves
2 teaspoons coriander seeds
1 teaspoon cumin seeds
1 teaspoon peppercorns
3 garlic cloves, sliced
About 1-1/4 cups olive oil

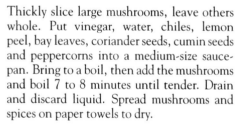

Thickly slice large mushrooms, leave others
whole. Put vinegar, water, chiles, lemon
peel, bay leaves, coriander seeds, cumin seeds
and peppercorns into a medium-size saucepan. Bring to a boil, then add the mushrooms
and boil 7 to 8 minutes until tender. Drain
and discard liquid. Spread mushrooms and
spices on paper towels to dry.

Fill a 2-1/2 cup canning jar with boiling
water, pour out water and place jar in a warm
oven to dry. Fill jar with mushroom mixture
and garlic slices. Add oil, making sure mushrooms are completely covered. Seal tightly
and marinate 5 days in the refrigerator.

Makes about 2-1/2 cups.

MARINATED OLIVES

2-3/4 cups ripe olives (1 pound)
1 fresh red chile, seeded, chopped
3 garlic cloves, chopped
2 thyme sprigs
2 tablespoons dill seeds, lightly crushed
Salt and freshly ground pepper
Olive oil to cover
2 tablespoons chopped dill

Using a small sharp knife make a lengthwise
slit through to the pit of each olive.

Put olives in a bowl with chile, garlic, thyme
and dill seeds. Season with salt and freshly
ground pepper. Add enough olive oil to just
cover. Cover bowl and refrigerate 3 to 14
days.

Drain olives; reserve oil for cooking or salad
dressings. Discard thyme sprigs. Serve olives
sprinkled with chopped dill.

Makes 6 servings.

– SPINACH WITH GORGONZOLA –

2 red bell peppers
About 4 ounces young spinach leaves
1 head Belgium endive
1 ripe pear
1/3 cup crumbled Gorgonzola cheese
DRESSING:
3 tablespoons extra-virgin olive oil
1 tablespoon lemon juice
1 garlic clove, crushed
2 tablespoons chopped Italian parsley
Salt and freshly ground pepper

Preheat broiler. Cook whole peppers under hot broiler about 10 minutes, turning occasionally, until skins are evenly blistered and blackened. Transfer peppers to a plastic bag a few minutes and then peel away and discard skins. Cut peppers in half, remove and discard seeds, and cut peppers into strips. Place in a salad bowl.

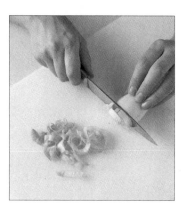

Tear spinach leaves into bite-size pieces; slice endive. Peel core and slice pear. Add spinach, endive and pear to salad bowl. Mix all dressing ingredients together in a small bowl or put in a jar with a tight-fitting lid and shake until blended. Pour over salad and toss to mix. Scatter Gorgonzola cheese over salad and serve immediately.

Makes 4 to 6 servings.

FAVA BEANS IN TOMATO SAUCE

6 tablespoons olive oil
2 garlic cloves, chopped
1 small onion, finely chopped
2 sage sprigs
2 pounds fresh fava beans, shelled
1 (14-oz.) can chopped plum tomatoes
1 tablespoon sun-dried tomato paste
Salt and freshly ground pepper
Sage leaves to garnish

Heat oil in a large heavy saucepan. Add garlic, onion and sage sprigs and cook 4 to 5 minutes to soften.

Stir in beans, tomatoes and tomato paste and bring to a boil. Reduce heat, cover and cook 20 minutes, stirring frequently, until beans are tender. Discard sage sprigs and season with salt and freshly ground pepper. Serve hot garnished with sage leaves.

Makes 4 to 6 servings.

DEEP-FRIED SMALL FISH

8 ounces small fish such as anchovies and young
    sardines
1/2 cup all-purpose flour
2 teaspoons finely chopped Italian parsley
Salt and freshly ground pepper
Peanut oil for deep-frying
Lemon slices to serve

Rinse fish thoroughly, drain and pat dry on
paper towels.

Put flour, parsley, salt and freshly ground
pepper into a plastic or paper bag and shake to
mix. Add fish in batches and shake gently to
coat.

Half-fill a deep-fryer or saucepan with oil and
preheat to 350F (175C). Deep-fry the fish in
batches in the hot oil 2 to 3 minutes until
golden-brown. Drain on paper towels. Serve
hot with lemon slices.

Makes 4 servings.

Note: The fish are eaten whole so it is necessary to choose only those which are small
enough not to require cleaning.

──MUSSEL & FENNEL SALAD──

3 pounds mussels in their shells
1 garlic clove, chopped
1/4 cup water
1 medium-size fennel bulb
1 small onion, sliced
Salt and freshly ground pepper
1/3 cup extra-virgin olive oil
Juice of 1 lemon

Scrub mussels, rinse thoroughly and remove beards. Discard any that do not close when tapped firmly. Put mussels into a large sauce-pan with the garlic and water. Cover and cook on high heat about 5 minutes until shells open.

Drain and reserve 2 tablespoons of the cooking liquid. Discard any unopened mussels. Cool mussels. Trim fennel, reserving any feathery tops to garnish. Cut fennel bulb into matchsticks. Place in a serving dish with onion.

Remove and discard shells from most of the mussels leaving about 12 to 16 mussels in shells; reserve mussels in shells for garnish. Add shelled mussels to serving dish with the reserved cooking liquid. Season with salt and freshly ground pepper. Drizzle olive oil and lemon juice over mussels and toss to mix. Serve sprinkled with the chopped fennel tops and garnished with the mussels in shells.

Makes 4 to 6 servings.

STUFFED MUSSELS

3 pounds large mussels in their shells
1/3 cup dry white wine
1/2 cup fresh bread crumbs
1/3 cup olive oil
3 tablespoons chopped Italian parsley
1 tablespoon finely chopped oregano or 1 teaspoon
   dried leaf oregano
2 garlic cloves, crushed
Salt and freshly ground pepper
Lemon slices and Italian parsley leaves to garnish

Scrub mussels and remove beards. Discard any that do not close when tapped firmly. Put in a large saucepan with white wine.

Cover and boil 4 to 5 minutes, until shells open. Strain, reserving liquid. Discard any unopened mussels. Remove and discard half of each shell leaving mussels on remaining halves. Mix together bread crumbs, half of the olive oil, the herbs, garlic, salt and pepper. If mixture is dry add a little of the reserved mussel juice to moisten.

Preheat broiler. Divide bread crumb mixture among mussels and arrange on baking sheets. Sprinkle with remaining olive oil and cook under medium-hot broiler 1 to 2 minutes until the crumb mixture is crisp and golden. Serve hot garnished with lemon slices and parsley leaves.

Makes 4 to 6 servings.

——MINTY SEAFOOD SALAD——

2/3 cup dry white wine
1 shallot, chopped
5 peppercorns
1/3 cup water
1 pound shelled scallops, fresh or frozen and thawed
1 pound cooked large shrimp
4 celery stalks
2 medium-size carrots
About 16 mint leaves
1/2 teaspoon finely grated lemon peel
DRESSING:
Juice of 2 lemons
1/2 cup extra-virgin olive oil
1 tablespoon white wine vinegar
2 tablespoons chopped Italian parsley
Salt and freshly ground pepper

Put white wine, shallot, peppercorns and water in a shallow pan. Heat until boiling then add scallops. Reduce heat and poach 5 to 6 minutes, until scallops are just firm and opaque. Using a slotted spoon transfer scallops to paper towels to drain and cool. Discard cooking liquid. Slice scallops in half horizontally. Put in a serving dish. Peel shrimp and add to dish.

Cut celery and carrots into thin matchsticks and add to seafood with mint leaves and lemon peel. Toss lightly to mix. To make dressing, mix ingredients together in a small bowl or put in a jar with a tight-fitting lid and shake until blended. Pour over salad and toss. Cover and refrigerate 30 minutes before serving.

Makes 4 to 6 servings.

SQUID SALAD

1 pound small or medium-size squid
1-1/4 cups dry white wine
1 shallot, chopped
Strip of lemon peel
1 garlic clove, chopped
1 red onion, chopped
1/4 cup chopped mixed fresh herbs such as basil,
    tarragon and Italian parsley
Fresh herb sprigs to garnish
DRESSING:
5 tablespoons extra-virgin olive oil
2 tablespoons lemon juice
1 teaspoon balsamic vinegar
1 teaspoon Dijon-style mustard
Salt and freshly ground pepper

Clean squid (see page 61). If very small leave whole, otherwise slice into rings. Put wine, shallot, lemon peel and garlic into a medium-size saucepan. Bring to a boil and boil 1 minute. Add the squid, in batches if necessary, and cook 5 to 7 minutes until firm but still tender. Using a slotted spoon, remove to a serving dish and cool.

Add onion and the herbs to the squid and toss to mix. To make dressing, mix all ingredients together in a small bowl, or shake together in a jar with a tight-fitting lid. Pour over salad and toss to mix. Cover and refrigerate at least 30 minutes before serving. Garnish with fresh herb sprigs.

Makes 4 servings.

——SCALLOPS WITH GARLIC——

12 large sea scallops, on the half shell
1/4 cup extra-virgin olive oil
2 garlic cloves, chopped
2 tablespoons chopped Italian parsley
1/3 cup dry white wine
Juice of 1 lemon
Salt and freshly ground pepper
Lemon slices and parsley sprigs to garnish

Remove scallops from their shells and rinse under cold running water. Drain on paper towels. Clean 6 scallop shells thoroughly and set aside in a warm oven for serving.

Heat oil in a skillet. Add garlic and parsley and cook 1 minute. Reduce heat and stir in scallops. Season with salt and freshly ground pepper, cover and cook 5 minutes, stirring twice. Stir wine into pan, and cook, covered, 3 minutes. Remove lid, increase heat and cook 4 to 5 minutes to reduce liquid by half. Remove from heat.

Add lemon juice to pan and stir well. Adjust seasoning and divide scallops among the reserved scallop shells. Divide cooking liquid among them. Serve immediately garnished with lemon slices and parsley sprigs.

Makes 4 to 6 servings.

FRIED SARDINE FILLETS

1-1/2 pounds small fresh sardines, scaled
2 eggs
2 cups dried bread crumbs
1 tablespoon finely chopped oregano or 1 teaspoon
    dried leaf oregano
1 tablespoon finely chopped Italian parsley
Salt and freshly ground pepper
Peanut oil for deep-frying
Lemon slices to serve

Remove heads from sardines and slit each fish along stomach. Clean thoroughly. Lay each fish cut-side down on a board. Press firmly along backbone to loosen, then turn fish over and lift away bones.

Beat eggs in a shallow dish. In a separate shallow dish mix bread crumbs, herbs and seasoning.

Half-fill a deep-fryer with oil and preheat to 350F (175C). Dip each sardine fillet into beaten egg, then into bread crumb mixture to coat. Deep-fry sardines, two at a time, in the hot oil about 4 minutes until golden-brown. Drain on paper towels. Serve at once with lemon slices.

Makes 4 servings.

— DEEP-FRIED SQUID & SHRIMP —

8 ounces medium-size squid
12 ounces large shrimp
About 1/2 cup all-purpose flour
1 teaspoon salt
Peanut oil for deep-frying
Lemon wedges to serve
Italian parsley sprigs to garnish

Clean and prepare squid (see page 61). Slice body parts into rings. Peel and devein shrimp.

Put flour in a shallow dish and season with salt and freshly ground pepper. Roll squid and shrimp in seasoned flour to coat.

Half-fill a deep-fryer or saucepan with oil and preheat to 350F (175C). Add a few pieces of fish at a time to hot oil and deep-fry about 3 minutes until golden. Using a slotted spoon transfer to paper towels to drain. Serve immediately with lemon wedges. Garnish with Italian parsley sprigs.

Makes 4 servings.

MIXED SEAFOOD SALAD

2/3 cup dry white wine
2/3 cup water
Juice of 1/2 lemon
1 shallot, chopped
8 parsley sprigs, separated into stalks and leaves
2 garlic cloves, chopped
1-1/2 pounds prepared raw seafood such as squid,
    clams, mussels and large unpeeled shrimp or shucked
    scallops
Scant 1 cup mayonnaise
1/2 teaspoon finely grated lemon peel
1 head lettuce, separated into leaves
Lemon slices to garnish
Salt and freshly ground pepper

Put wine, water, lemon juice, shallot, parsley stalks and 1 garlic clove in a large pan. Bring to a boil and boil 1 minute. Add prepared seafood according to length of cooking time of each type, starting with those that need longest cooking. (Allow 15 minutes for squid, 5 to 6 minutes for shrimp, 4 to 5 minutes for scallops, 2 to 3 minutes for mussels and clams.) Using a slotted spoon, transfer cooked pieces to a large bowl.

Strain cooking liquid into the bowl and cool. Cover and refrigerate at least 1 hour.

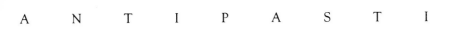

Chop parsley leaves with remaining garlic clove.

Put garlic and parsley into a bowl and stir in mayonnaise and lemon peel. Season with salt and freshly ground pepper. Transfer to a serving bowl.

Arrange lettuce leaves on a plate. Drain seafood and pile into center of plate. Season and garnish with lemon slices. Serve mayonnaise separately.

Makes 4 to 6 servings.

HOT ANCHOVY DIP

2 (1-3/4-oz.) cans anchovy fillets, drained and coarsely chopped
1-1/4 cups whipping cream
2 garlic cloves, crushed
4 tablespoons unsalted butter, diced
TO SERVE:
Cubes of crusty bread
Bread sticks
Vegetables pieces for dipping such as fennel, celery, bell peppers, radishes, endive and broccoli
Italian parsley leaves to garnish

Put anchovies in a small saucepan with cream and garlic. Bring to a boil, then reduce heat and simmer, uncovered and stirring occasionally, 12 to 15 minutes until smooth and thickened.

Stir in butter. Transfer to a serving dish. Garnish with Italian parsley leaves and serve with cubes of bread, bread sticks and vegetables.

Makes 4 servings.

Note: Traditionally, the serving dish is kept hot at the table like a fondue over a candle or burner.

—TUNA-STUFFED TOMATOES—

8 medium-size firm but ripe tomatoes
1 red onion, finely chopped
1 garlic clove, crushed
2 tablespoons chopped Italian parsley
2 tablespoons chopped basil or 2 teaspoons dried leaf
   basil
3 tablespoons extra-virgin olive oil
2 teaspoons red wine vinegar
1 (7-oz.) can tuna in olive oil, drained and flaked
Salt and freshly ground pepper
Mixed lettuce leaves to serve
Basil leaves to garnish

Slice tops off tomatoes and discard. Using a teaspoon, carefully scoop out seeds and flesh from tomatoes. Set tomatoes aside; reserve pulp and seeds for use in sauce.

In a bowl, mix together onion, garlic, parsley, basil, olive oil and vinegar. Add tuna, salt and pepper, and stir lightly to mix. Divide among tomatoes. Cover and refrigerate at least 1 hour before serving. Serve with lettuce leaves. Garnish with basil leaves.

Makes 4 servings.

——— SHRIMP WITH MELON ———

12 cooked jumbo shrimp
1 small Charentais or cantaloupe melon
1 small Galia melon
Juice of 1 small lemon
Salt and freshly ground pepper
Mint leaves to garnish

Peel shrimp leaving the tail tips on, if desired.

Cut melons into thin wedges and remove skins.

Arrange shrimp and the two different colored varieties of melon on a platter or individual plates and sprinkle with lemon juice. Season with salt and freshly ground pepper. Serve garnished with mint leaves.

Makes 4 to 6 servings.

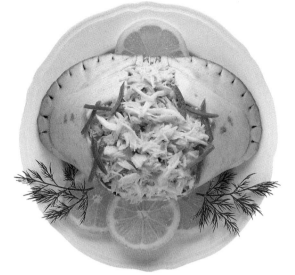

DRESSED CRAB

2 cooked crab (about 2-1/8 pounds each)
1/4 cup extra-virgin olive oil
Juice of 1 lemon
Salt and freshly ground pepper
TO GARNISH:
1 red bell pepper packed in wine vinegar, drained, cut
    into strips
Lemon slices
Italian parsley or fennel sprigs

Remove large claws and legs from crabs. Crack open with a small hammer and remove flesh. Flake into a bowl.

Pry open one body and remove any white meat and all the brown meat from body shells, discarding the mouth part, grey stomach sacks and feathery gills. Add all the crabmeat to the bowl. Scrub shell clean. Repeat with other crab.

Sprinkle olive oil and lemon juice over crabmeat and season with salt and freshly ground pepper. Mix together lightly with a fork. Pile meat back into crab shells and serve cold garnished with bell pepper strips, lemon slices and parsley or fennel sprigs.

Makes 4 servings.

—— MARINATED RAW FISH ——

1 pound very fresh red mullet or sardines, ready to cook
1 garlic clove, finely chopped
Juice of 2 lemons
1/2 red onion, finely chopped
1/4 teaspoon hot red pepper flakes
1/4 cup extra-virgin olive oil
Salt and freshly ground pepper
1 teaspoon chopped Italian parsley and Italian parsley
    sprig to garnish

Remove heads, tails, fins and backbones (see page 50) of fish. Wash fillets and pat dry. Arrange in one layer in a shallow dish.

Sprinkle with garlic and add the juice of 1-1/2 lemons. Cover and refrigerate 24 hours, turning fish once.

Drain fish thoroughly and arrange in a serving dish. Sprinkle with onion and hot pepper flakes. Add remaining lemon juice and olive oil and season with salt and freshly ground pepper. Serve sprinkled with chopped Italian parsley. Garnish with Italian parsley sprig.

Makes 4 servings.

Note: It is important to use fish that is very fresh as it is cooked only by the acid in the lemon juice.

TUNA SALAD

3 small carrots, thickly sliced
1-1/3 cups diced potatoes (about 8 ounces)
1 (7-oz.) can tuna in olive oil, drained and flaked
1 (1-3/4-oz.) can anchovy fillets in oil, drained and
   chopped
About 12 pitted ripe olives, halved
2 tablespoons capers in wine vinegar, drained
2 hard-cooked eggs, quartered
1/4 cup extra-virgin olive oil
Juice of 1 small lemon
1 garlic clove, crushed
Salt and freshly ground pepper
1 tablespoon chopped Italian parsley
Italian parsley sprigs to garnish

Cook carrots in a saucepan of boiling salted water 4 minutes until tender. Cook potatoes in a separate saucepan of boiling salted water about 7 minutes until tender. Drain and refresh both vegetables under cold running water, then drain and cool completely.

Put carrots, potatoes, tuna, anchovies, olives, capers and eggs into a large serving dish. Mix olive oil, lemon juice, garlic and salt and pepper together in a small bowl or put in a jar with a tight-fitting lid and shake until blended. Pour over salad, toss lightly to mix, then sprinkle with chopped Italian parsley. Garnish with Italian parsley sprigs.

Makes 4 servings.

–CRABMEAT & SHRIMP TOASTS–

1 cup flaked white crabmeat
3/4 cup peeled cooked shrimp
2 teaspoons lemon juice
2 tablespoons butter
1/4 cup all-purpose flour
1-1/4 cups milk
2 tablespoons marsala wine
1/2 teaspoon Dijon-style mustard
1 tablespoon chopped Italian parsley
2 tablespoons whipping cream
Salt and freshly ground pepper
4 slices crusty white bread to serve
Italian parsley sprigs and lemon slices to garnish

Put crabmeat, shrimp and lemon juice into a small bowl and mix lightly. Melt butter in a small saucepan. Stir in flour and cook, stirring, 1 minute. Remove from heat, then gradually beat in milk. Return to the heat and bring to a boil, stirring constantly. Reduce heat and simmer 5 minutes, stirring frequently.

Stir in marsala and mustard, then remove from the heat and lightly fold in parsley, cream and the crabmeat mixture. Season with salt and freshly ground pepper. Toast bread, place on plates and top with hot mixture. Garnish with parsley sprigs and lemon slices.

Makes 4 servings.

STUFFED SQUID

1-1/2 to 2 pounds squid
4 anchovy fillets canned in oil, drained
1 garlic clove, crushed
1 tablespoon dried bread crumbs
1/3 cup pine nuts, toasted and coarsely chopped
1 tablespoon chopped Italian parsley
2 teaspoons chopped fennel
1 egg, beaten
Salt and freshly ground pepper
3 tablespoons extra-virgin olive oil
Juice of 1/2 lemon
Fennel and lemon slices to garnish

Preheat oven to 350F (175C). To prepare squid, pull head away from body pouch.

Discard viscera that come away with it. Pull quill-shaped pen free from pouch and discard. Cut head away from the tentacles and discard head. Squeeze out beaklike mouth from in between the tentacles and discard. Rinse pouch and tentacles thoroughly under cold running water. Cook tentacles in boiling salted water 5 minutes, then drain and chop finely. Place in a bowl. Add anchovies and mash with a fork. Stir in garlic, bread crumbs, pine nuts and herbs. Mix in egg and season with freshly ground pepper.

Stuff squid with bread crumb mixture and secure openings with wooden picks. Arrange stuffed squid in one layer in a shallow oven-proof dish. Sprinkle with olive oil and lemon juice. Bake in preheated oven 45 to 60 minutes until tender. Serve garnished with fennel and slices of lemon.

Makes 4 to 6 servings.

FRIED SHRIMP

1 pound extra-large shrimp
1/4 cup extra-virgin olive oil
2 garlic cloves, crushed
1 small fresh green chile, seeded and sliced
2 tablespoons chopped Italian parsley
1 to 2 tablespoons anise liqueur
Salt and freshly ground pepper
Lemon wedges to garnish

Remove and discard heads and legs from shrimp.

Heat oil in a large skillet. Add garlic, chile and shrimp; fry quickly 2 to 3 minutes until shrimp turn bright pink.

Stir in parsley and liqueur; season with salt and freshly ground pepper. Serve at once garnished with lemon wedges.

Makes 4 servings.

———— BUTTERFLIED SHRIMP ————

1 pound extra-large shrimp
Juice of 1 lemon
5 tablespoons extra-virgin olive oil
1/2 garlic clove, crushed
2 teaspoons sun-dried tomato paste
Pinch of red (cayenne) pepper
1 tablespoon chopped basil or 1 teaspoon dried leaf basil
Salt and freshly ground pepper
Basil sprigs to garnish

Remove and discard heads and legs from shrimp. Using sharp scissors, cut shrimp lengthwise almost in half, leaving tail end intact.

Place shrimp in a shallow dish and add half of the lemon juice and 2 tablespoons of the olive oil. Stir in garlic. Cover and marinate at least 30 minutes. Preheat broiler. Arrange shrimp in 1 layer on a rack and cook under hot broiler about 3 minutes until shrimp have curled and are bright pink.

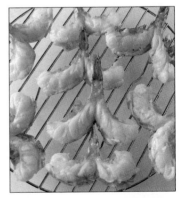

Mix together the remaining lemon juice and the 3 tablespoons olive oil, the sun-dried tomato paste, cayenne, basil, salt and freshly ground pepper in a small bowl. Either spoon over shrimp or serve separately for dipping. Garnish shrimp with basil sprigs.

Makes 4 servings.

TUNA PATE

3 tablespoons butter
4 green onions, white part only, chopped
2 celery stalks, finely chopped
1 (7-oz.) can tuna in water, drained
2 tomatoes, peeled, seeded and chopped
2 tablespoons mayonnaise
1 teaspoon lemon juice
1 teaspoon white wine vinegar
Salt and freshly ground pepper
Chopped Italian parsley, parsley leaves and pitted green
    olives to garnish
Crusty bread or toast to serve

Melt butter in a small skillet over low heat. Add green onions and celery; cook 5 minutes to soften. Let cool.

Put green onion mixture in a blender or food processor with remaining ingredients, except garnish and bread. Process until fairly smooth. Transfer to a serving dish, cover and refrigerate at least 30 minutes. Garnish with chopped parsley, parsley leaves and green olives and serve with crusty bread or toast.

Makes 4 to 6 servings.

STUFFED ONIONS

4 large onions
8 ounces ground veal
2 slices bacon, finely chopped
1/3 cup shredded provolone cheese
1 or 2 garlic cloves, crushed
1 tablespoon sun-dried tomato paste
1 tablespoon finely chopped Italian parsley
1 tablespoon chopped oregano or 1 teaspoon dried leaf
  oregano
1 small egg, beaten
Salt and freshly ground pepper
Fresh Italian parsley sprigs or oregano sprigs to garnish

Grease a baking dish. Peel onions and place in a large saucepan, cover with water and bring to a boil. Cook 25 to 30 minutes until just tender. Drain and cool slightly. Preheat oven to 400F (205C). Cut onions in half horizontally. Using a teaspoon, carefully remove centers of onions, leaving shells about 3 layers thick. Use pieces from the centers to cover any holes in the bottoms; discard remaining centers.

Mix together remaining ingredients, except garnish, in a small bowl. Divide among onion shells and arrange them in the baking dish. Bake in preheated oven 40 to 45 minutes until filling is cooked through. Serve hot garnished with Italian parsley or oregano sprigs.

Makes 4 servings.

BRESAOLA SALAD

16 slices bresaola
Mixed lettuce leaves
4 large fresh basil leaves, shredded
DRESSING:
3 tablespoons extra-virgin olive oil
1/4 teaspoon finely grated lemon peel
Juice of 1/2 lemon
Salt and freshly ground pepper
Basil leaves and lemon slices to garnish

Arrange bresaola and lettuce leaves on individual serving plates or a large platter. Sprinkle with shredded basil leaves.

In a small bowl, mix together olive oil, lemon peel and lemon juice and spoon over bresaola and lettuce. Season with salt and freshly ground pepper. Garnish with basil leaves and lemon slices.

Makes 4 servings.

— VENETIAN CHICKEN SALAD —

1/4 cup raisins
Juice of 1 orange
1/3 cup pine nuts
1 pound cooked chicken breast, cut into strips
Small pinch of ground cloves
1/3 cup extra-virgin olive oil
1 tablespoon white wine vinegar
1 to 2 teaspoons balsamic vinegar
Salt and freshly ground pepper
Mixed lettuce leaves to serve

Heat raisins and orange juice to boiling in a small saucepan. Remove from heat. Let stand 20 minutes. Drain and set aside raisins; discard liquid.

Put pine nuts into a small saucepan or skillet, without oil; place over medium heat and stir 3 minutes until golden.

Put pine nuts and all other ingredients, except lettuce, into a bowl and toss well to mix. Cover and refrigerate 30 minutes. Serve with lettuce leaves.

Makes 4 to 6 servings.

——— PROSCIUTTO WITH FIGS ———

12 paper-thin slices prosciutto
4 to 6 ripe figs
Fresh Italian parsley leaves or mint sprigs to garnish

Arrange prosciutto on a platter or individual plates.

Halve figs lengthwise, then cut into quarters, and arrange beside ham. Serve garnished with parsley leaves or mint sprigs.

Makes 4 servings.

— BRESAOLA & CHEESE ROLLS —

4 ounces dolcelatte cheese
2 ounces mascarpone cheese
Salt and freshly ground pepper
12 thin slices bresaola
Mixed lettuce leaves
Juice of 1 lemon
3 tablespoons extra-virgin olive oil
Lemon slices to garnish

In a small bowl mix together dolcelatte and mascarpone cheeses until well blended. Season with salt and freshly ground pepper.

Lay bresaola slices flat on a board. Divide mixture among slices and roll up.

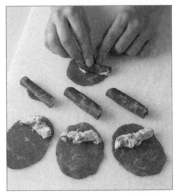

Arrange lettuce leaves on a platter or individual plates and place the bresaola rolls on top. Sprinkle with lemon juice and olive oil and a little more pepper. Serve garnished with lemon slices.

Makes 4 servings.

MORTADELLA SALAD

1 (8-oz.) piece mortadella sausage
1 small red onion, sliced
1/2 each yellow and red bell peppers packed in wine
    vinegar, drained
3 small sweet dill pickles, sliced
6 radishes, sliced
12 pitted green olives, halved
6 leaves romaine lettuce
DRESSING:
1/4 cup extra-virgin olive oil
2 tablespoons red wine vinegar
1 teaspoon Dijon-style mustard
1 tablespoon chopped Italian parsley
Salt and freshly ground pepper

Cut mortadella into 1/2-inch cubes and place
in a bowl with onion. Cut yellow and red bell
peppers into strips and add to bowl with dill
pickles, radishes and olives.

To make dressing, mix all ingredients
together in a small bowl, or shake together in
a jar with a tight-fitting lid. Pour over salad
and toss to mix. Tear lettuce leaves into
pieces and arrange on a serving plate. Place
salad on top and serve at once.

Makes 4 to 6 servings.

POLLO FRITTO

1 pound chicken breast and thigh meat
3 tablespoons olive oil
Juice of 1/2 lemon
1 garlic clove, crushed
About 1/2 cup all-purpose flour
2 eggs, beaten
2 cups dried bread crumbs
1 teaspoon paprika
Salt and freshly ground pepper
Peanut oil or light olive oil for deep-frying
Lemon wedges and Italian parsley leaves to garnish

Cut chicken into 2-inch pieces and place in a shallow dish. Add the 3 tablespoons olive oil, lemon juice and garlic and stir well. Cover and marinate at least 1 hour. Put flour into a shallow dish. Put eggs into a second shallow dish, and mix together bread crumbs, paprika and seasoning in a third dish. Drain chicken. Coat a few pieces at a time first in flour, then eggs, then in seasoned bread crumb mixture.

Half-fill a deep-fat fryer with oil, and preheat to 350F (175C). Deep-fry coated chicken pieces, in batches, about 3 minutes, turning once, until crisp and golden. Serve hot garnished with lemon wedges and parsley leaves.

Makes 4 servings.

CARPACCIO

1 (10-oz.) piece beef tenderloin
1 (3-oz.) piece Parmesan cheese, thinly sliced
3 cups thinly sliced button mushrooms (8 ounces)
Leaves from about 8 Italian parsley sprigs
DRESSING:
1/2 cup extra-virgin olive oil
Juice of 2 lemons
1 garlic clove, chopped
Salt and freshly ground pepper

Put beef in freezer 30 minutes. Using a very sharp knife, cut beef into wafer-thin slices.

Lay beef slices in the center of a large serving plate and arrange Parmesan slices, mushrooms and parsley around edge.

To make dressing, whisk ingredients together in a small bowl or put in a jar with a tight-fitting lid and shake until thoroughly blended. Pour over beef, cheese, mushrooms and parsley.

Makes 6 servings.

──── ITALIAN MEAT PLATTER ────

4 ounces thinly sliced mixed salamis
2 ounces thinly sliced mortadella
2 ounces thinly sliced prosciutto or coppa
2 ounces thinly sliced bresaola
2 large pickles
1 small bunch radishes, trimmed
6 ounces cherry tomatoes
3/4 cup ripe olives or green olives
Lettuce leaves
Italian parsley leaves to garnish
DRESSING:
5 tablespoons extra-virgin olive oil
2 tablespoons lemon juice
1 tablespoon red wine vinegar
1 teaspoon Dijon-style mustard
Salt and freshly ground pepper

Arrange meats on a large platter. Thinly slice pickles on the diagonal and add to platter with radishes, tomatoes, olives and lettuce leaves.

To make dressing, mix all ingredients together in a small bowl and serve with meat platter. Garnish with parsley leaves.

Makes 6 to 8 servings.

Note: The selection of meats can be varied to include your favorites. Serve with crusty bread, bread rolls or bread sticks.

—VEAL & SPINACH TERRINE—

1 pound fresh spinach
1 pound ground veal
4 slices bacon, finely chopped
3/4 cup shredded provolone cheese (3 ounces)
1/2 cup fresh bread crumbs
1 tablespoon chopped Italian parsley
2 eggs, beaten
Salt and freshly ground pepper
Italian parsley sprigs to garnish

Preheat oven to 325F (165C). Grease and line bottom of a 9″ × 5″ loaf pan with waxed paper. Rinse spinach thoroughly; do not dry. Cook in a large saucepan without additional water about 2 minutes until wilted. Transfer to a colander and press out excess water using a wooden spoon. Chop finely.

In a large bowl, mix together spinach and remaining ingredients, except parsley sprigs. Spoon into the loaf pan and smooth the top Cover with oiled foil and cook in preheated oven 1 to 1-1/4 hours until firm. Remove from oven, cool slightly, then refrigerate in pan until cold. Turn out and slice; garnish with parsley sprigs.

Makes 6 servings.

PORK & LIVER PATE

12 ounces bacon slices
8 ounces lean pork, chopped
8 ounces pork liver, chopped
8 ounces pork sausage
1 small onion, finely chopped
2 garlic cloves, chopped
1 tablespoon chopped thyme
1 tablespoon chopped oregano
3 tablespoons marsala wine
Salt and freshly ground pepper
Thyme and oregano sprigs to garnish

Preheat oven to 325F (165C). Grease an 8″ × 4″ loaf pan. Lay bacon slices flat on a board and stretch using the back of a knife.

Line the loaf pan, with the bacon slices, reserving a few slices to cover the top. Place pork in a blender or food processor and process until finely chopped. Add remaining ingredients and process briefly until well blended but not smooth. Put pork mixture into loaf pan, smooth top and cover with reserved bacon. Cover tightly with oiled foil.

Place loaf pan in a roasting pan half-filled with boiling water. Cook in preheated oven 1-1/2 to 1-3/4 hours until firm. Remove foil. Cover pate with waxed paper, then put a plate or board and a heavy weight on top; refrigerate overnight before turning out. Slice to serve and garnish with herb sprigs.

Makes 6 to 8 servings.

——BRESAOLA & PEAR SALAD——

2 ripe pears
8 slices bresaola
1/2 head leaf lettuce
Italian parsley sprigs to garnish
DRESSING:
2 ounces dolcelatte cheese
2 tablespoons peanut oil
1 tablespoon lemon juice
1/2 teaspoon Dijon-style mustard
1/2 to 1 teaspoon sugar
3 tablespoons half and half
Salt and freshly ground pepper

To make dressing, put cheese in a small bowl. Using a fork, mash cheese, then gradually beat in oil and lemon juice until smooth. Beat in remaining ingredients.

Peel and core pears and cut lengthwise into thin slices. Arrange on a serving plate or individual plates with bresaola and lettuce. Serve immediately with the dressing. Garnish with parsley sprigs.

Makes 4 servings.

—CHICKEN & GRAPE SALAD—

1 pound cooked chicken breasts
1-1/4 cups walnut halves
1 cup seedless green grapes, halved
16 stuffed green olives, sliced
3 green onions, sliced
Salt and freshly ground pepper
1 head romaine lettuce, separated into leaves
DRESSING:
2/3 cup mayonnaise
1 garlic clove, chopped
1 teaspoon paprika
2 tablespoons chopped Italian parsley
Few drops of hot pepper sauce
2 tablespoons milk

Cut chicken into thin strips, and place in a bowl with walnuts, grapes, olives and green onions. Season with salt and freshly ground pepper.

To make dressing, mix all ingredients together in a small bowl. Pour over salad and toss gently to mix. Arrange lettuce on a serving plate. Pile chicken salad in center and serve at once.

Makes 4 to 6 servings.

-ITALIAN SAUSAGES & LENTILS-

2 cups green lentils
2 tablespoons extra-virgin olive oil
2 slices bacon, chopped
1 onion, finely chopped
2 garlic cloves, crushed
2 celery stalks, finely chopped
Salt and freshly ground pepper
4 to 6 fresh spicy Italian pork sausages
Chopped Italian parsley and parsley sprigs to garnish

Put lentils in a bowl, cover with cold water
and soak 2 hours. Drain.

Heat 1 tablespoon of the oil in a large saucepan. Add bacon, onion, garlic and celery;
cook 3 to 4 minutes until beginning to
brown. Add lentils and enough water to just
cover. Bring to a boil, reduce heat and simmer 25 minutes until lentils are tender,
adding a little more water if necessary. Season
with salt and freshly ground pepper.

Meanwhile, in a skillet, fry sausages in the
remaining 1 tablespoon oil about 10 minutes,
turning occasionally, until evenly browned.
Thickly slice sausages. Spoon lentils onto a
warmed serving plate, place sausage slices on
top and sprinkle with chopped parsley and
garnish with parsley sprigs.

Makes 4 to 6 servings.

—— SAUTEED LAMB KIDNEYS ——

12 lamb kidneys
2 tablespoons butter
1 tablespoon olive oil
2 garlic cloves, crushed
1 small onion, finely chopped
1 teaspoon whole-grain mustard
1/4 cup marsala wine
Salt and freshly ground pepper
Hot toasted bread to serve
Chopped Italian parsley and parsley sprigs to garnish

Remove and discard the thin membrane surrounding kidneys. Cut each in half. Using kitchen scissors, snip out white cores.

Heat butter and oil in a large skillet. Add garlic and onion and saute 3 minutes until just softened. Add kidneys and cook over high heat, stirring, 2 to 3 minutes until browned but still tender.

Stir mustard and marsala into pan and cook 1 minute. Season with salt and freshly ground pepper. Serve on hot toasted bread and sprinkle with chopped Italian parsley and garnish with parsley sprigs.

Makes 4 to 6 servings.

FRITTO MISTO

About 3/4 cup all-purpose flour
Salt and freshly ground pepper
2 eggs, beaten
About 2 cups dry bread crumbs
4 lamb kidneys, halved and cored
8 ounces calves' liver, cut into strips
8 ounces fresh spicy Italian sausages, cut into bite-size
    pieces
1 small eggplant, sliced
2 medium-size zucchini, thickly sliced
Vegetable oil for deep-frying
Italian parsley sprigs to garnish

Put flour into a shallow dish; season with salt
and freshly ground pepper. Put eggs into a
second shallow dish and bread crumbs into a
third dish. Dip kidneys, liver, sausages, eggplant and zucchini first in seasoned flour,
then in eggs and finally in bread crumbs to
coat evenly.

Half-fill a deep-fat fryer with oil. Preheat to
350F (175C). Deep-fry meats and vegetables,
in batches, 2 to 4 minutes, turning once,
until crisp and golden. Using a slotted spoon,
transfer to paper towels to drain. Serve hot
garnished with parsley sprigs.

Makes 6 to 8 servings.

CHICKEN LIVER TOASTS

3 tablespoons olive oil
1 celery stalk, finely chopped
2 garlic cloves, crushed
8 ounces chicken livers, chopped
1 teaspoon chopped fresh sage
1/4 cup marsala wine
2 anchovy fillets canned in oil, drained
1 tablespoon capers in wine vinegar, drained
Freshly ground pepper
1 medium-size loaf French bread
Capers and fresh sage leaves to garnish

Preheat oven to 375F (190C). Heat oil in a large skillet. Add celery and garlic and cook 2 minutes to soften.

Add chicken livers and fry over high heat about 3 minutes, stirring occasionally, until crisp and brown on outside but still pink inside. Using a wooden spoon, stir in sage and marsala, scraping up all the cooking juices. Transfer to a blender or food processor and add anchovy fillets and capers. Season with freshly ground pepper and process until fairly smooth. Transfer to a warmed plate, cover and place over a saucepan of hot water to keep warm.

Cut bread diagonally into thick slices and lay on a baking sheet. Bake in preheated oven 6 to 7 minutes until golden. Serve the chicken liver paste on the baked bread, and garnish with capers and sage leaves.

Makes 6 to 8 servings.

– CHICKEN WITH GREEN SAUCE –

1 pound cooked chicken breasts
Mixed lettuce leaves
Italian parsley sprigs to garnish
SAUCE:
1 bunch Italian parsley
8 basil sprigs
1 (1-3/4-oz.) can anchovy fillets in oil, drained
1 shallot, chopped
2 garlic cloves, crushed
3 tablespoons white wine vinegar
1 teaspoon Dijon-style mustard
1/4 cup fresh bread crumbs
Freshly ground pepper
1/2 cup extra-virgin olive oil

To make sauce, using a blender or food pro-cessor, process all sauce ingredients, except olive oil, to a smooth paste. With motor running, slowly pour in oil to make a thick but pourable consistency.

Slice the chicken and arrange with lettuce leaves on a serving plate or individual plates. Pour sauce over and around the chicken. Garnish with parsley sprigs.

Makes 4 to 6 servings.

——— BRANDIED LIVER PATE ———

8 ounces calves' liver
8 ounces chicken livers
1/2 cup butter
Rosemary sprig
1 bay leaf
5 tablespoons brandy
Salt and freshly ground pepper
Rosemary sprigs to garnish

Discard any veins from livers. Dice calves' liver, and cut chicken livers in half.

Melt 2 tablespoons of the butter in a large skillet, add rosemary, bay leaf and chicken livers and cook over high heat 3 minutes, stirring occasionally, until crisp on the outside but still pink inside. Remove to a blender or food processor and set aside. Add calves' liver to the pan and cook over high heat about 3 minutes. Add to chicken livers. Using a wooden spoon, stir 2 tablespoons of the brandy into pan scraping up the cooking juices.

Discard herbs from pan, then pour cooking juices into the blender or food processor; process until smooth. Transfer to a bowl, and cool. Beat in remaining butter and brandy. Season with salt and freshly ground pepper. Transfer to a serving dish, cover and refrigerate a few hours until firm. Serve garnished with rosemary sprigs.

Makes 4 servings.

EGGS WITH ANCHOVY DRESSING

3 ounces arugula or other lettuce leaves
4 hard-cooked eggs, halved
1 teaspoon finely chopped Italian parsley
1 teaspoon snipped fresh chives
ANCHOVY DRESSING:
5 anchovy fillets canned in oil, drained
1/3 cup mayonnaise
3 to 4 tablespoons milk
Freshly ground pepper

To make dressing, put anchovy fillets in a small bowl. Mash with a fork, then blend in mayonnaise, adding milk to give a creamy consistency. Season with freshly ground pepper.

Arrange lettuce leaves and egg halves on a serving plate. Spoon dressing over and around eggs and sprinkle with herbs.

Makes 4 servings.

FRITTATA

1 large russet potato, about 10 ounces
2 tablespoons butter
2 tablespoons vegetable oil
1 small onion, chopped
1 red bell pepper, diced
3 tablespoons chopped fresh herbs such as basil,
   oregano, mint, parsley, sage or thyme
4 eggs, beaten
Salt and freshly ground pepper
Fresh herb sprigs and lettuce leaves to garnish

Cut potatoes into 1-inch pieces. Boil in salted water 12 to 15 minutes until tender. Drain thoroughly, then mash; set aside.

Heat half of the butter and half of the oil in a large skillet over low heat. Add onion and bell pepper and cook 5 minutes to soften, but do not brown. Add to mashed potatoes with herbs and eggs. Season with salt and freshly ground pepper.

Preheat broiler. Heat remaining butter and oil in a large nonstick skillet. Add potato mixture, spreading it evenly with a spatula. Cook over medium heat about 4 minutes until the bottom is set and lightly browned. Put under the hot broiler until the top of the frittata is set and golden. Serve hot or cold cut into wedges and garnished with fresh herb sprigs and lettuce leaves.

Makes 4 to 6 servings.

—PEPPERED PECORINO CHEESE—

1 pound pecorino cheese
3 tablespoons peppercorns, lightly crushed
1 teaspoon finely grated lemon peel (optional)
2/3 cup extra-virgin olive oil
Italian parsley sprig to garnish

Remove rind from cheese and discard. Cut cheese into 1-inch cubes. Put into a shallow dish.

Sprinkle peppercorns and lemon peel, if using, over cheese. Add oil.

Cover dish with foil and refrigerate 2 hours, basting cheese occasionally. Remove from refrigerator 30 minutes before serving. Garnish with parsley sprig.

Makes 6 to 8 servings.

Note: This dish can be kept covered in the refrigerator up to 4 days, but it is important to return it to room temperature 30 minutes before serving.

MOZZARELLA FRITTERS

1 pound mozzarella cheese
3/4 cup all-purpose flour
1 teaspoon paprika
Salt and freshly ground pepper
2 eggs, beaten
2 cups dried bread crumbs
Peanut oil or vegetable oil for deep-frying
Sage leaves to garnish

Cut mozzarella cheese into 1-1/2-inch cubes. Mix flour, paprika, salt and freshly ground pepper in a shallow dish. Put eggs into a second shallow dish and bread crumbs into a third dish.

Coat cheese cubes lightly in the seasoned flour. Dip into eggs, then into bread crumbs to coat evenly. Repeat once more with eggs and bread crumbs.

Half-fill a deep-fat fryer with oil. Preheat to 350F (175C). Deep-fry a few cheese cubes at a time about 2 minutes until golden. Using a slotted spoon, transfer to paper towels to drain. Serve hot garnished with sage leaves.

Makes 4 to 6 servings.

——— EGG & WALNUT SALAD ———

1 head leaf lettuce
6 tomatoes, coarsely chopped
1/2 red onion, thinly sliced
16 pitted ripe olives, halved
1/3 cup walnut pieces
4 hard-cooked eggs, quartered
1 tablespoon chopped fennel tops
1 tablespoon snipped fresh chives
DRESSING:
3 tablespoons extra-virgin olive oil
2 tablespoons walnut oil
2 tablespoons red wine vinegar
1 teaspoon whole-grain mustard
Pinch of sugar
Salt and freshly ground pepper

Tear lettuce into bite-size pieces and put in a salad bowl with tomatoes, onion, olives, walnuts, eggs and herbs. Toss gently to mix.

To make dressing, mix all ingredients together in a small bowl, or shake together in a jar with a tight-fitting lid. Pour over salad and serve at once.

Makes 4 to 6 servings.

ITALIAN CHEESE DIP

1/2 red bell pepper
1/2 yellow bell pepper
2 ounces dolcelatte cheese
2 ounces mascarpone cheese
1 tablespoon lemon juice
2 small dill pickles, finely chopped
Salt and freshly ground pepper
Breadsticks, page 118, and a selection of cooked and
    raw vegetables to serve

Preheat broiler. Cook bell peppers skin-side up under the hot broiler 5 to 7 minutes, until skins are evenly blistered and charred. Transfer to a plastic bag a few minutes and then peel away and discard skins. Finely chop flesh and set aside.

Put dolcelatte cheese in a small bowl and mash with a fork. Mix in mascarpone cheese and lemon juice until blended, then fold in the chopped bell peppers and dill pickles. Season with salt and freshly ground pepper. Serve with Breadsticks and a selection of cooked and raw vegetables.

Makes 4 servings.

—POACHED EGGS FLORENTINE—

4 eggs
2 tablespoons white wine vinegar
2 tablespoons butter
12 ounces spinach leaves, rinsed and finely shredded
1/3 cup whipping cream
2 tablespoons Dijon-style mustard
2 teaspoons chopped Italian parsley
Salt and freshly ground pepper
Hot buttered toast to serve
Paprika and Italian parsley sprigs to garnish

Preheat the oven to 250F (120C). To poach eggs, fill a large saucepan with water to a depth of 2 inches. Add vinegar and bring to a boil. Reduce heat to low. Crack an egg onto a saucer and slide egg into pan. Repeat with another egg. Poach 2 eggs at a time 3 to 4 minutes until cooked as desired. Using a slotted spoon, transfer to a warmed plate and put on lowest shelf in the warm oven. Cook remaining 2 eggs in same way, add to plate and place in the warm oven.

Melt butter in a saucepan. Add spinach and cook, stirring, 1 to 2 minutes until just wilted. Drain off any excess liquid, then stir in remaining ingredients except toast and garnish. Serve spinach and poached eggs accompanied by hot buttered toast. Sprinkle eggs with paprika and garnish with Italian parsley sprigs.

Makes 4 servings.

—BAKED EGGS WITH RICOTTA—

2 tablespoons butter, melted
1/2 cup ricotta cheese
2 teaspoons snipped fresh chives
4 eggs
1/4 cup whipping cream
Salt and freshly ground pepper
Whole chives to garnish

Preheat oven to 350F (175C). Use butter to grease 4 small individual heatproof dishes. Divide ricotta cheese among dishes, levelling surface with a teaspoon. Sprinkle cheese with chives.

Break an egg into each dish and top with cream. Season with salt and freshly ground pepper.

Place dishes in a shallow baking pan half-filled with warm water. Bake in preheated oven 10 to 12 minutes until eggs are cooked as desired. Garnish with whole chives.

Makes 4 servings.

FONDUTA

1 pound fontina cheese, diced
1-1/4 cups milk
1/4 cup unsalted butter, melted
4 large egg yolks
Freshly ground pepper
Breadsticks, page 118, crusty bread or toast for dipping
Italian parsley sprig to garnish

Place cheese and milk in a bowl. Refrigerate at least 2 hours to soften. Transfer to a double boiler or heatproof bowl set over a pan of simmering water; heat until cheese melts and becomes stringy. Stir in butter and remove from heat.

Beat egg yolks in a small bowl. Stir in a little of the hot cheese mixture, then pour back into the remaining cheese mixture. Return to the heat and beat vigorously until smooth, creamy and thickened. Season with freshly ground pepper.

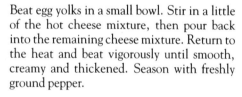

Transfer to a serving dish (the dish is usually kept hot at table over a candle or small burner), and serve with Breadsticks, crusty bread or toast for dipping. Garnish with parsley sprig.

Makes 6 servings.

Note: If fontina cheese is not available a mixture of 8 ounces Gruyere cheese and 8 ounces Edam cheese is a good substitute.

——————— STUFFED EGGS ———————

6 eggs
1/3 cup soft cheese with garlic and herbs (3 ounces)
3 tablespoons half and half
1 tablespoon snipped fresh chives
Salt and freshly ground pepper
Sliced ripe olives and chives to garnish
Mixed lettuce leaves to serve

Place eggs in a medium-size saucepan. Cover with water and bring to a boil. Reduce heat and simmer about 10 minutes until hard-cooked.

Drain eggs and place under cold running water until cool. Peel eggs; cut in half lengthwise. Remove yolks from eggs, and put into a small bowl. Mash with a fork.

Add cheese, half and half and chives and mix until smooth. Season with salt and freshly ground pepper. Spoon or pipe into egg whites and garnish with ripe olives and chives. Serve with lettuce leaves.

Makes 4 to 6 servings.

MOZZARELLA SALAD

1 pound mozzarella cheese
2 red onions, thinly sliced
1 tablespoon chopped Italian parsley
1 tablespoon chopped basil or 1 teaspoon dried leaf basil
1 tablespoon snipped fresh chives
1 teaspoon chopped mint
1 (1-3/4-oz.) can anchovy fillets in oil, drained
Italian parsley sprig to garnish
DRESSING:
5 tablespoons extra-virgin olive oil
1 tablespoon white wine vinegar
1 teaspoon balsamic vinegar
1/2 garlic clove, crushed
Salt and freshly ground pepper

Cut mozzarella cheese into slices. Arrange onions on a large plate or individual plates. Arrange cheese on top.

Sprinkle chopped herbs over cheese. To make dressing, mix all ingredients together in a small bowl, or shake in a jar with a tight-fitting lid. Pour over salad. Arrange anchovy fillets on cheese and herbs in a lattice pattern and serve at once garnished with parsley sprig.

Makes 4 to 6 servings.

EGG & OLIVE SALAD

1 pound small new potatoes
3 hard-cooked eggs, halved or quartered
1/2 head romaine lettuce
18 pitted ripe olives, halved
Salt and freshly ground pepper
1/3 cup mayonnaise
1 (1-3/4-oz.) can anchovy fillets in oil, drained
Paprika to garnish

Cook potatoes in boiling, salted water 12 to 15 minutes until tender. Drain and cool completely.

Halve or quarter potatoes and arrange with eggs, lettuce and olives on a serving plate or individual plates. Season with salt and freshly ground pepper.

Spoon mayonnaise over salad and arrange anchovy fillets on top. Sprinkle with a little paprika. Refrigerate 1 hour before serving.

Makes 6 servings.

—MARINATED SOFT CHEESE—

3/4 cup ricotta cheese (6 ounces)
6 ounces cream cheese, softened
8 Italian parsley sprigs, coarsely chopped
8 basil sprigs
1 tablespoon chopped oregano or 1 teaspoon dried leaf oregano
2 garlic cloves, chopped
1/4 teaspoon hot pepper flakes
Juice of 1/2 lemon
10 peppercorns, lightly crushed
2/3 cup extra-virgin olive oil
Fresh grape leaves to serve (optional)
Oregano sprigs to garnish

In a small bowl, beat cheeses together with a wooden spoon. Divide into 6 portions and shape into balls or round cakes. Arrange in 1 layer in an oiled shallow dish. Using a blender or food processor, process remaining ingredients, except grape leaves, until fairly smooth.

Pour over cheeses. Cover dish with foil and refrigerate 3 hours, basting cheeses occasionally. Remove from refrigerator 30 minutes before serving on a bed of grape leaves, if using. Garnish with oregano sprigs.

Makes 6 servings.

Note: If available, 1-1/2 cups Italian straccino or robiola can replace the cheeses in the recipe.

RICOTTA MOLDS

1-1/2 cups ricotta cheese (12 ounces)
1 tablespoon finely chopped Italian parsley
1 tablespoon chopped fennel tops
1 tablespoon snipped fresh chives
1 tablespoon unflavored gelatin powder
3 tablespoons water
2/3 cup mayonnaise
Salt and freshly ground pepper
Fresh herb sprigs to garnish
BELL PEPPER SAUCE:
2 large red bell peppers, broiled, peeled and chopped,
    page 14
3 tablespoons extra-virgin olive oil
Few drops of balsamic vinegar
Salt and freshly ground pepper

In a bowl, mix together cheese and herbs. Oil 6 (about 1/2-cup) molds. In a small bowl, soften gelatin in water 5 minutes. Place bowl over a saucepan of simmering water and stir until dissolved. Cool slightly, then stir into cheese mixture with mayonnaise, salt and freshly ground pepper. Divide among oiled molds, cover and refrigerate until set.

To make sauce, put bell peppers and oil in a food processor or blender and process until smooth. Add balsamic vinegar to taste, and season with salt and freshly ground pepper. Pour into a small bowl, and refrigerate until required. Turn out ricotta molds onto individual plates and serve with sauce. Garnish with herb sprigs.

Makes 6 servings.

STUFFED CHILES

12 fresh red or green chiles
3 tablespoons extra-virgin olive oil
1 tablespoon white wine vinegar
Mint leaves to garnish
FILLING:
4 sun-dried tomatoes in oil, drained and finely chopped
5 ounces mild soft goat cheese
2 green onions, white part only, finely chopped
2 teaspoons finely chopped mint
1 teaspoon finely chopped basil or 1/3 teaspoon dried
   leaf basil
Salt and freshly ground pepper
Mint leaves to garnish

Preheat broiler. Cook chiles under hot broiler 8 to 10 minutes, turning occasionally, until skins are evenly blistered and charred. Transfer to a plastic bag a few minutes, then peel away and discard skins. Make a lengthwise cut down length of each chile. Carefully rinse out seeds under cold running water. Pat the chiles dry with paper towels.

To make filling, mix ingredients together in a small bowl. Divide filling among chiles and arrange on a serving plate. Drizzle with olive oil and vinegar. Cover and refrigerate at least 30 minutes. Garnish with mint leaves.

Makes 4 to 6 servings.

FAVA BEANS WITH GOAT CHEESE

1/4 cup extra-virgin olive oil
1 onion, chopped
2 pounds fresh fava beans, shelled, or 12 ounces frozen
  fava beans, thawed
1 tablespoon chopped rosemary
Salt and freshly ground pepper
2 heads Belgian endive or 1 head radicchio
1 (8-oz.) goat cheese log, sliced
Rosemary sprigs to garnish

Heat oil in a large skillet, add onion and cook over medium heat about 10 minutes until soft and golden. Stir in beans and rosemary.

Add enough water to just cover beans and season with salt and freshly ground pepper. Bring to a boil, reduce heat, cover and simmer 12 to 15 minutes, stirring frequently, until beans are very tender and liquid is absorbed.

Preheat broiler. Slice endive or radicchio and stir into hot beans. Lay cheese slices on top of bean mixture. Put skillet under hot broiler 2 to 3 minutes until cheese is browned. Serve hot garnished with rosemary sprigs.

Makes 4 to 6 servings.

BELL PEPPER PIZZETTES

PIZZA DOUGH:
4 cups bread flour or all-purpose flour
Pinch of salt
1 (1/4-oz.) package active dry yeast (about
    1 tablespoon)
1 teaspoon sugar
Scant 1 cup warm water (110F, 45C)
2 tablespoons extra-virgin olive oil
Oregano sprigs to garnish
TOPPING:
2 red or yellow bell peppers
3 tablespoons sun-dried tomato paste
1/4 cup capers in wine vinegar, drained
2 tablespoons chopped fresh oregano or 2 teaspoons
    dried leaf oregano
Salt and freshly ground pepper

Sift flour and salt into a large bowl. In a small bowl, dissolve yeast and sugar in water. Let stand 5 to 10 minutes until frothy. Stir in olive oil. Using a wooden spoon, gradually stir yeast mixture into flour to give a soft, but not sticky, dough. Knead on a floured surface 5 minutes until smooth and elastic. Place in an oiled medium-size bowl, cover and let rise in a warm place 35 to 40 minutes until doubled in size.

Meanwhile, preheat broiler. Cook bell peppers under hot broiler about 10 minutes, turning occasionally, until skins are evenly blistered and charred. Transfer peppers to a plastic bag a few minutes, then peel away and discard skins. Cut peppers into strips. Set aside.

Preheat oven to 450F (230C). Oil 2 baking sheets. Turn out dough onto a lightly floured surface. Knead gently and cut into 16 equal pieces. Roll each piece into a small oval about 1/4 inch thick.

Transfer to the baking sheets and prick dough with a fork. Divide sun-dried tomato paste, reserved peppers, capers and oregano among dough ovals. Season with salt and freshly ground pepper. Bake in preheated oven 8 to 10 minutes until golden. Serve hot or warm garnished with oregano sprigs.

Makes 16 pizzettes.

Red Onion & Gorgonzola Pizzettes In place of above topping, use 1-1/2 cups (4 ounces) crumbled Gorgonzola cheese, 1/2 chopped red onion and 2 tablespoons chopped thyme.

Shrimp & Fennel Pizzettes Replace bell peppers, capers and herbs with 1 small roasted fennel bulb, 4 ounces cooked shrimp and 2 teaspoons fennel seeds. To roast fennel, brush with olive oil and place in a preheated 350F (175C) oven 35 to 40 minutes. Cool and chop.

FOCACCIA

4 cups bread flour or all-purpose flour
Pinch of salt
1 (1/4-oz.) package active dry yeast (about 1
  tablespoon)
1 teaspoon sugar
1 cup warm milk (110F, 45C)
1/4 cup extra-virgin olive oil, plus extra for brushing
2 teaspoons rosemary
Coarse sea salt

Sift flour and salt into a large bowl.

In a small bowl, dissolve yeast and sugar in
milk. Let stand 5 to 10 minutes until frothy.
Stir in the 1/4 cup olive oil. Using a wooden
spoon, gradually beat yeast mixture into flour
mixture to give a soft, but not sticky, dough.
Knead on a lightly floured surface 5 minutes
until smooth and elastic. Place in an oiled
medium-size bowl, cover and let rise in a
warm place about 40 minutes until doubled in
size. Turn out onto a lightly floured surface
and knead 5 minutes.

Oil a baking sheet. Roll out dough to a large
circle about 1/2 inch thick and transfer to
baking sheet. Brush dough with olive oil,
sprinkle with rosemary and sea salt and
lightly press into surface. With your finger
make deep indentations over surface. Let rise
25 minutes. Preheat oven to 450F (230C).
Bake in preheated oven 20 to 25 minutes
until golden. Brush again with olive oil.
Serve warm.

Makes 1 loaf.

BREAD SALAD

8 ounces firm, country-style bread, crusts removed
1 red onion, thinly sliced
1/2 cucumber, peeled and diced
6 small tomatoes, quartered
2 celery stalks, sliced
6 basil sprigs, shredded
9 pitted ripe olives, halved
Salt and freshly ground pepper
5 tablespoons extra-virgin olive oil
2 tablespoons red wine vinegar
1 teaspoon balsamic vinegar

Cut bread into small cubes and place in a large bowl. Sprinkle with enough cold water to moisten thoroughly but do not let bread become soggy.

Add onion, cucumber, tomatoes, celery, shredded basil and olives to bowl. Season with salt and freshly ground pepper. In a small bowl, mix together oil and vinegars, then pour over salad. Toss well to mix. Let stand 30 minutes before serving.

Makes 6 servings.

——TOMATO & ONION BREAD——

4 cups bread flour or all-purpose flour
Pinch of salt
1 (1/4-oz.) package active dry yeast (about
   1 tablespoon)
1 teaspoon sugar
Scant 1 cup warm water (110F, 45C)
4 tablespoons extra-virgin olive oil
1 onion, finely chopped
1 garlic clove, crushed
4 ounces sun-dried tomatoes preserved in oil, drained
9 large basil leaves
Freshly ground pepper
Milk to glaze
1 teaspoon coarse sea salt
Basil leaves to garnish

Sift flour and salt into a large bowl. In a small bowl, dissolve yeast and sugar in warm water. Let stand 5 to 10 minutes until frothy.

Stir 3 tablespoons of the olive oil into yeast mixture. Using a wooden spoon, gradually stir yeast mixture into flour to give a soft, but not sticky, dough. Knead on a lightly floured surface 5 minutes until smooth and elastic. Put dough into an oiled medium-size bowl, cover and let rise in a warm place 35 to 40 minutes until doubled in size.

Oil a baking sheet, Heat remaining 1 table-spoon oil in a skillet, add onion and garlic, and cook 3 minutes until softened. Remove skillet from heat and set aside. Turn out dough onto a lightly floured surface and cut in half. Roll out to give 2 rectangles each about 12" × 9". Transfer 1 piece to the baking sheet and prick surface with a fork.

Spread cooked onion mixture over pricked dough, leaving a 1/2-inch border around the edge. Arrange sun-dried tomatoes and basil leaves over onion and season with freshly ground pepper. Moisten edges of dough with a little cold water and cover with second sheet of dough.

Crimp dough edges to seal. Using a sharp knife mark a lattice pattern on surface of dough. Brush with a little milk to glaze and sprinkle with coarse sea salt. Let rise 20 minutes. Preheat oven to 450F (230C). Bake loaf in preheated oven about 25 minutes until golden-brown and underside is firm and lightly colored. Serve warm or cold, on its own as part of the antipasti. Cut into pieces and garnish with basil leaves.

Makes 1 large loaf.

GOAT CHEESE TARTS

1 to 2 teaspoons extra-virgin olive oil
2 tablespoons butter
2 cups fresh bread crumbs
1 tablespoon sesame seeds
6 ounces goat cheese
4 sun-dried tomatoes preserved in oil, drained
Salt and freshly ground pepper
4 basil leaves
1 teaspoon finely chopped mint
Mixed lettuce leaves and chives to garnish

Preneat oven to 400F (205C). Use olive oil to grease 4 (3- to 4-inch) tart pans.

Melt butter in a small saucepan, and stir in bread crumbs and sesame seeds. Divide among prepared tart pans, pressing firmly onto bottoms and sides. Bake in preheated oven 12 to 15 minutes until crisp and light golden. Carefully remove tart shells from pans and place on a baking sheet.

Divide goat cheese among tart shells and top each with a sun-dried tomato. Season with salt and freshly ground pepper. Return to oven 8 to 10 minutes to heat through. Put a basil leaf and a sprinkling of chopped mint on each tart and garnish with mixed lettuce leaves and chives.

Makes 4 servings.

—BRUSCHETTA AL POMODORO—

8 small thick slices rustic bread
1/4 cup extra-virgin olive oil
1 garlic clove, crushed
2 large tomatoes, chopped
2 tablespoons chopped basil or 2 teaspoons dried leaf
   basil
Salt and freshly ground pepper
8 anchovy fillets canned in oil, drained (optional)

Preheat oven to 400F (205C). Put bread in 1 layer on a baking sheet. Bake in preheated oven 10 minutes until golden.

Meanwhile warm oil and garlic in a small saucepan.

Drizzle oil and garlic over bread. Divide tomatoes and basil among slices, season with salt and freshly ground pepper and top with anchovy fillets, if using. Serve at once.

Makes 4 servings.

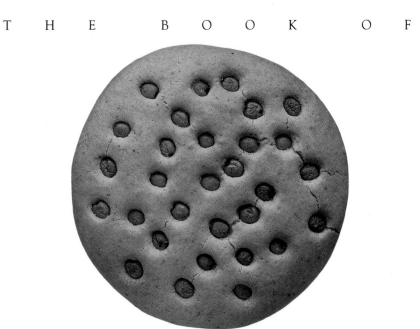

——————— OLIVE BREAD ———————

1 (1/4-oz.) package active dried yeast (about
   1 tablespoon)
1 teaspoon sugar
1-1/3 cups warm water (110F, 45C)
6 cups bread flour or all-purpose flour
Pinch of salt
1 tablespoon chopped oregano or 1 teaspoon dried leaf
   oregano
1/4 cup extra-virgin olive oil, plus extra for brushing
30 pitted green olives

In a small bowl, dissolve yeast and sugar in
warm water. Let stand 5 to 10 minutes until
frothy.

Sift flour and salt into a large bowl, and stir in
oregano. Stir olive oil into yeast mixture.
Using a wooden spoon, gradually stir yeast
mixture into flour to give a soft, but not
sticky, dough. Add a little more warm water
if necessary.

Knead dough on a lightly floured surface 5
minutes until elastic. Place in an oiled large
bowl, cover and let rise in a warm place about
40 minutes until doubled in size.

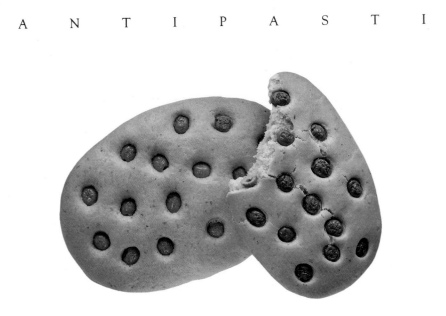

Grease 1 large baking sheet, or 2 smaller baking sheets. Turn out dough onto a floured surface. To make 1 large loaf, roll out to a large circle 1 inch thick. Or, cut dough in half and roll out 2 ovals about 1/2 inch thick. Place on the baking sheet or sheets.

With your floured finger, make 30 deep indentations over surface of large loaf, or 15 in each of the smaller ones. Press an olive into each indentation.

Brush with olive oil and let rise 25 minutes. Preheat oven to 450F (230C). Bake loaves in preheated oven 20 to 25 minutes for small loaves, 30 to 35 minutes for large loaf until golden-brown and undersides sound hollow when tapped. Cool on a wire rack. Serve warm or cold as part of the antipasti.

Makes 1 large or 2 small loaves.

——CRAB & RICOTTA TARTS——

PASTRY DOUGH:
2 cups all-purpose flour
Pinch of salt
1/2 cup butter, chilled, diced
About 1/4 water
FILLING:
8 ounces crabmeat
1 cup ricotta cheese (8 ounces)
3 green onions, finely chopped
2 whole eggs plus 1 yolk
2 tablespoons chopped Italian parsley
Few drops of hot pepper sauce
Salt and freshly ground pepper
Mixed lettuce leaves to serve
Italian parsley sprigs to garnish

Preheat oven to 400F (205C). Sift flour and salt into a small bowl. Rub in butter until mixture resembles bread crumbs. Stir in enough water to make a firm dough. Place dough on a floured surface and knead gently until smooth. Use to line 4 (3- to 4-inch) tart pans. Prick bottoms lightly and chill 20 minutes. Line tart shells with waxed paper and cover with dry beans. Bake in preheated oven 15 minutes, removing beans and paper after 10 minutes.

Remove tart shells from oven and reduce temperature to 350F (175C). To make filling, mix ingredients together in a bowl. Spoon into tart shells. Bake about 20 minutes until set and golden-brown. Serve warm or cold garnished with mixed lettuce leaves and parsley sprigs.

Makes 4 servings.

SAVORY PASTRIES

1 recipe Pizza Dough, page 100
Vegetable oil for deep-frying
FILLING:
3 tablespoons sun-dried tomato paste
2 tablespoons Olive Paste, page 115
6 ounces mozzarella cheese, thinly sliced
Freshly ground pepper
1 egg white, lightly beaten
Italian parsley sprigs to garnish

Make dough and let rise until doubled in size. On a lightly floured surface, roll out dough to 1/4 inch thick. Cut out circles using a 4-inch plain round cutter. Spread a little sun-dried tomato paste and Olive Paste onto each round of dough. Cut cheese slices in half and place a piece on each dough circle. Season and freshly ground pepper.

Brush edges of dough circles with a little egg white, then fold dough over filling to make half-moon shapes; press edges together to seal. Half-fill a deep-fat fryer with oil. Preheat to 350F (175C). Deep-fry a few pastries at a time, 2 to 3 minutes, turning once, until golden. Using a slotted spoon, transfer to paper towels to drain. Serve hot garnished with parsley sprigs.

Makes about 12.

WALNUT BREAD

1 (1/4-oz.) package active dry yeast
1 tablespoon honey
2/3 cup warm milk (110F, 45C)
3 cups bread flour or all-purpose flour
3 cups whole-wheat flour
1-1/2 teaspoons salt
2 tablespoons butter, diced
1-1/4 cups chopped walnuts
2 teaspoons fennel seeds, lightly crushed
1/2 teaspoon grated nutmeg
About 1 cup warm water
Milk to glaze

In a small bowl, dissolve yeast and honey in milk. Let stand 5 to 10 minutes until frothy.

Sift flours and salt into a large bowl. Rub butter into flour. Stir in walnuts, 1 teaspoon of the fennel seeds and the grated nutmeg.

Using a wooden spoon, stir yeast mixture into flour mixture, then gradually beat in enough water to form a soft, but not sticky, dough.

Knead dough on a lightly floured surface 5 minutes until elastic. Put dough into an oiled large bowl, cover and let rise in a warm place 35 to 40 minutes until doubled in size. Turn out onto a lightly floured surface and knead 5 minutes.

Preheat oven to 425F (220C). Oil a 6-inch round pan. Divide dough into 7 equal pieces and shape into balls. Arrange balls in oiled pan. Brush tops with milk and sprinkle with remaining 1 teaspoon fennel seeds. Let rise in a warm place 25 minutes. Bake in preheated oven about 45 minutes until browned and bottom sounds hollow when tapped.

Turn bread out onto a wire rack and cool. Serve as part of the antipasti.

Makes 1 large loaf.

Note: This bread is delicious served with cheese and fish dishes, for soaking up olive oil dressings and is particularly good toasted.

MOZZARELLA TOASTS

12 thick slices French or Italian bread
1/3 cup extra-virgin olive oil
1 teaspoon finely chopped Italian parsley
14 anchovy fillets canned in oil, drained
1 pound mozzarella cheese, cut into 12 slices
Freshly ground pepper
Italian parsley sprigs to garnish

Preheat broiler. Arrange bread in 1 layer on a baking sheet, then toast both sides under preheated broiler until golden.

Meanwhile put oil, parsley and 2 of the anchovy fillets in a small saucepan. Heat gently to warm, stirring with a fork to break up anchovies. Drizzle oil mixture over toasted bread and put a slice of cheese on each one. Season with freshly ground pepper.

Garnish with remaining anchovy fillets and return to broiler 2 to 3 minutes until cheese is hot and bubbling. Serve at once garnished with Italian parsley sprigs.

Makes 6 servings.

OLIVE PASTE TOASTS

4 large thick slices rustic bread
3 tablespoons extra-virgin olive oil
1/2 garlic clove, crushed
Red bell pepper strips and thyme sprigs to garnish
OLIVE PASTE:
1-1/4 cups pitted ripe olives (6 ounces)
2 tablespoons extra-virgin olive oil
Few drops of balsamic vinegar
Freshly ground pepper

Preheat oven to 400F (205C). To make Olive Paste, put ingredients in a food processor or blender and process until fairly smooth. Transfer to a bowl and set aside.

Cut each slice of bread into 3 strips. Place on a baking sheet and bake in preheated oven 10 to 12 minutes until golden and crisp. Meanwhile, warm oil with garlic in a small saucepan.

Drizzle oil and garlic over toasted bread. Spread with Olive Paste and serve at once garnished with bell pepper strips and thyme sprigs.

Makes 4 to 6 servings.

Note: Olive Paste can be made in advance or in larger quantities. Put into jars, add olive oil to cover and seal. Cover jars and keep in refrigerator up to 1 month.

MUSHROOM TART

2 cups all-purpose flour
Pinch salt
1/2 cup butter, chilled, diced
About 5 tablespoons water
FILLING:
1 ounce dried porcini mushrooms
2 tablespoons butter
1 medium-size onion, finely chopped
4 ounces button mushrooms, chopped
2 tablespoons finely chopped Italian parsley
1 tablespoon sun-dried tomato paste
1/4 cup half and half
3 large eggs
1/4 cup freshly grated Parmesan cheese (3/4 ounce)
Salt and freshly ground pepper
Italian parsley sprig to garnish

Sift flour and salt into a medium-size bowl. Rub butter in until mixture resembles bread crumbs. Stir in enough water to make a firm dough. Wrap in plastic wrap and refrigerate while preparing filling.

Preheat oven to 400F (205C). Grease a 9-inch pie pan. Put porcini in a small bowl. Cover generously with warm water. Let soak 20 minutes, then drain and rinse to remove any grit. Dry on paper towels, then chop finely and set aside.

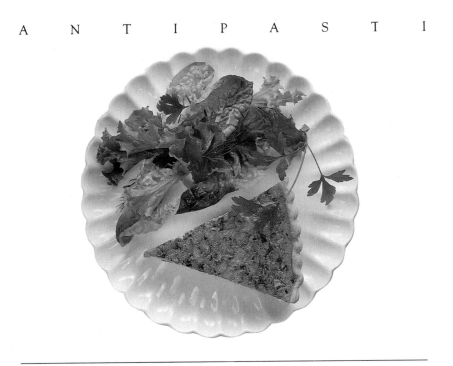

Melt butter in a medium-size saucepan. Add onion and button mushrooms and cook 5 minutes to soften. Stir in porcini mushrooms, parsley and sun-dried tomato paste. Cook 2 minutes, then stir in half and half. Cook over low heat 8 to 10 minutes until liquid is reduced by half. Remove from heat and cool.

Roll out the dough and use to line greased pie pan. Prick bottom with a fork. Line pie shell with waxed paper and fill with dry beans. Bake in preheated oven 25 minutes, removing beans and paper last 5 minutes. Reduce temperature to 375F (190C).

Beat eggs in a large bowl. Stir in mushroom mixture and cheese. Season with salt and freshly ground pepper, then pour into pie shell. Bake about 20 minutes until set. Serve warm or cold garnished with parsley sprig.

Makes 8 servings.

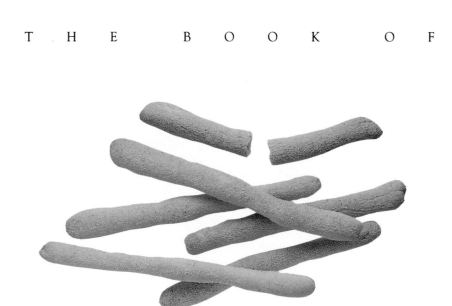

BREADSTICKS

4 cups bread flour or all-purpose flour
1/2 teaspoon salt
1/4 cup grated Parmesan cheese or provolone cheese
1 (1/4-oz.) package active dry yeast (about
   1 tablespoon)
1 teaspoon sugar
1-1/4 cups warm water (110F, 45C)
2 tablespoons extra-virgin olive oil plus extra for oiling
3/4 cup polenta or coarse cornmeal

Sift flour and salt into a large bowl. Stir in cheese. In a small bowl, dissolve yeast and sugar in warm water. Let stand 5 to 10 minutes until frothy.

Stir the 2 tablespoons olive oil into yeast mixture. Using a wooden spoon, gradually beat yeast mixture into flour to give a soft dough. Knead dough on a floured surface 5 minutes until smooth and elastic.

Lightly oil a baking sheet. Roll out dough to a large rectangle and transfer to the baking sheet. Brush surface with a little oil, cover loosely with plastic wrap and let rise in a warm place 35 to 40 minutes until doubled in size. Preheat oven to 450F (230C). Lightly oil 2 more baking sheets. Cut dough into 24 equal pieces. Sprinkle polenta or cornmeal onto work surface. Using your hands, roll each piece of dough into a long thin rope about 9 inches long, coating thoroughly in polenta or cornmeal.

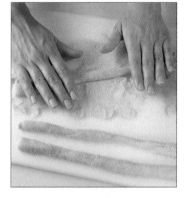

Arrange slightly apart on the baking sheets and bake in preheated oven 15 to 20 minutes until golden and crisp. Cool on wire racks. Serve warm or cold as part of the antipasti.

Makes 24 breadsticks.

Variation: Replace polenta or cornmeal with 3 ounces sesame seeds.

INDEX